Working copy

Commentary on the Gospel of Jesus According to Matthew

Pastor Ward Clinton

Copyright © 2016 Ward Clinton

All rights reserved.

ISBN10: 1508584052
ISBN-13: 978-1508584056

DEDICATION

To my wife

CONTENTS

Acknowledgments	i
Prelude to the Commentary	1
Chapter One	Pg 8
Chapter Two	Pg 25
Chapter Three	Pg 37
Chapter Four	Pg 55
Chapter Five	Pg 62
Chapter Six	Pg 93
Chapter Seven	Pg 119
Chapter Eight	Pg 133
Chapter Nine	Pg 146
Chapter Ten	Pg 157
Chapter Eleven	Pg 175
Chapter Twelve	Pg 189
Chapter Thirteen	Pg 198
Chapter Fourteen	Pg 205

ACKNOWLEDGMENTS

Thank you to my congregation which bore with and supported me throughout this whole process.

PRELUDE TO THE COMMENTARY

Peter, probably tried to encourage each one of the disciples to write a "memoir" but only three and the account written by Dr. Luke were actually commissioned by God to be part of His holy book. The so-called "lost gospels" were never lost, per se, but are fraudulent documents written by, in most, if not all, cases, someone other than whom they claim for themselves to have been written by and often at a different time than they claim for themselves.

Many have tried to assign a date of the writing of this gospel account after the destruction of the Temple in Jerusalem, which flies in the face of logic. In our day, the archaeologist's spade has provided us with very strong evidence that this gospel account was in wide circulation by 45 AD which also fits in well with the reliable testimony from some early church fathers. Some estimations that it may have been written as early as 36 AD don't currently have any solid evidence to support the claim but that is most certainly not outside the realm of possibility. Within a few days or weeks following Pentecost the Apostles may have already been thinking along the line of thought that some letters of instruction needed to be written for the new converts who did not have the privilege of being near enough to where the Apostles were residing to be properly instructed in the teaching which they themselves had been privileged to receive directly from Messiah Jesus. Remember, on the day of Pentecost there were 3,000 brand new converts and every one of them is going to need further assistance.

Personally I support the idea that before the year was out, following the resurrection, Peter's gospel account had already been written and was being carefully copied and distributed everywhere. As a result of its early authorship there were plenty of people around who were able to say "Hey, I was there when this particular thing happened and not only is the account accurate but let me tell you what else Jesus did that day."

The four gospels come first in the New Testament not necessarily because they were written before the Epistles but because they provide the proper transition from one section of the Scripture to the next. Furthermore, Matthew provides the most natural transition from that which is commonly called the Old Testament to that which is commonly called the New Testament. Matthew is a point of union between the two sections because it is the most Jewish of the four. Therefore, with Matthew sitting as the transition point, the Old Testament is not done away with but it is continued, clarified, and enhanced. The Old Testament looks forward to the coming of the Messiah while the New Testament proclaims He came and went but is coming back.

This gospel is of all four the one which bears the most evidentiary marks of having been prepared and constructed with a special view to the Jewish people. On that basis many scholars over the centuries have asserted it had to have been the first one to have been written while ignoring internal evidence which seems to clearly indicate otherwise. On the surface, it seems logical to believe it had to have been the first. On the other hand it certainly appears to have borrowed heavily from the Gospel of Jesus The Christ according to Mark, the secretary of Peter. For those who wish to stick with the idea that it was written completely independent of Mark, that is most assuredly within the realm of possibilities, as Peter and Matthew were both eyewitnesses to what Jesus said and did.

With its genealogy and birth account this gospel account does sit logically as the bridge between the two sections of the Holy Bible. A book to the Jews and for the Jews would seem to have to come before one addressed to gentile converts simply because the first followers of Jesus were all Jews and they remained rather orthodox in their religious practices even though they were being despised by many of those who had chosen to reject Jesus as their Messiah. Therefore, the reasoning follows, in part, that the disciples would not have targeted a book to the gentiles until much later.

How much later? Well certainly far less than is usually suggested since the centurion Cornelius was converted to Christianity between three to five years after the resurrection. By that time the Apostles are fully aware of the need for written instruction to guide folk in the way of Jesus the Nazarene as well as to accurately preserve His sayings. The church was also experiencing a quiet growth spurt because of a brief respite from persecution as the whole of Judaism was then focused on preventing Caligula's plan to erect his statue in Jerusalem and compel the Jews to offer sacrifices to it. Herod Agrippa, who was then at Rome, was trying to persuade Caligula not to commit the impious act and he was successful in that attempt although it took some months. It was probably just long enough for the Gospel accounts of Mark and Matthew to be written and to begin to be carefully copied and distributed among the believers. The sect of the Nazarene was still rigorously scrupulous in the observance of the Mosaic Law at that time.

Because of the harmony in the gospels there were some who tried to suggest a common source book from which the gospel writers drew. However, they simply failed to pay attention to what was setting right in front of them:

A. The Spirit of God moving upon holy men of God.
B. The Disciples were eye and ear witnesses to what Jesus said and did.
C. Early church fathers held that the Disciples left Jerusalem within twelve years following the resurrection and Peter and Matthew had already written their "memoirs".
D. Matthew, likely, had a copy of Mark at hand when he sat down to write his account as can be seen by the fact that he incorporates so much of it into his work.
E. If Matthew did not have a copy of Mark in hand as he wrote then see A and B above.

It may very well be that Matthew approached Peter and said something similar to, "I've been doing some research in the Temple archives and have traced Jesus' genealogy and you need to include it and maybe these few other things you left out." Peter gently (remember this is after Pentecost, when he is much better at these things) suggested that Matthew should write his own accounting however he saw fit because he, Matthew, was the one better suited to writing an account of the life and ministry of Jesus. After all, why would Cornelius and his family and friends realistically need to know all that stuff? A kinder yoke has been provided.

The chief characteristic of this Gospel is the representation of Jesus as the Messiah in whom was fulfilled the Law and the Prophets. Matthew's representation of Jesus as the Messiah is the result of careful consideration and he wrote in a spirit which was philosophical with a controversial element. He groups incidents and discourses together in a manner which illustrate who this Jesus is. He is controversial because he is challenging some false notions regarding the Messiah and His reign which was ruinous to the Jewish people. The best sort of controversy is that which is intent upon explaining the truth rather than focusing on exposing and ridiculing what is false. Therefore this evangelist presents Jesus as God's Anointed One. The manner, in which he records our Lord's urgent warnings against following false messiahs at the time when the destruction of Jerusalem should draw near, is a witness to the depth of his convictions.

Like the author of the Epistle to the Hebrews he cannot endure any thought of any waiverers or deserters. The Jewish Christian must be loyal to Jesus, even though the invasion of the holy city may sorely tempt him to throw in his lot with his patriotic but unbelieving kinsmen.

There is order and purpose in the arrangement of the groups of miracles and parables. The first miracle in this gospel account is the cure of leprosy, and is a symbol of sin being cleansed; while the last is the withering of the fig tree, which is a symbol of judgment. The first parable is that of the seed of the kingdom which is a symbol of the beginning or planting of the kingdom; the last is that of the talents and it prophesies the final adjudication at the last day.

It is a teaching gospel. While it tells us about a number of miracles, it is marked by several discourses, the Sermon on the Mount, chapters 3-7, the prophecy of the destruction of Jerusalem, and the end of the world, chapters 24-25, and the doctrines of the kingdom , chapters 17-20.

There are no songs of joy like those of Zacharias, Elizabeth, Mary, Simeon, Anna, and the angels which we find in Luke's gospel.

Matthew's account of the cross is one of desolation with no penitent thief or sympathy from anyone, with His enemies reviling Him as they passed by. Nor is there much optimism or expectation of success. The disciples are to be rejected even as their Lord was.

This is a Kingly Gospel. The genealogy demonstrates the royal descent of Jesus. The Magi came seeking Him that was "Born king of the Jews," John the Baptizer came preaching that the "Kingdom of Heaven is at hand."

In this gospel we find Jesus giving the gentiles a place in His kingdom, giving women a place in His kingdom. Too many American feminists foolishly view Christianity as oppressive and that is primarily because they have failed to comprehend and recognize the truly liberating aspects of Christianity. The idea of freedom and liberty for the common folk are Christian concepts.

It is a gospel of Jewish antagonism and rejection. On the one hand the Jews antagonize and reject Jesus. On the other the Jews, especially the Scribes and Pharisees, are exposed in their duplicities and rejected by Jesus because they rejected Him.

The Pharisees plotted against Jesus and resented His

violation of their regulations and customs concerning the Sabbath and their ceremonies about eating and washing and His associations with publicans and sinners (common people). They don't like the fact that Jesus won't let them "lord" it over Him. Jesus resents their violation of His rules, the actual Biblical ordinances, and points out their hypocrisy.

This is a Jewish Gospel. Jewish symbols, terms, and numbers are used without explanation as though Matthew expects his readers to be fully aware of their meaning. Jesus is for the Jews; Jesus is for the Gentiles; Jesus is for the women. Jesus is even for the Muslim, but only if they are willing to embrace the Truth and reject the false.

Jesus said unto him, I am the way, the truth, and the life: no man cometh unto the Father, but by me. – John 14:6

He that believeth on him [Jesus] is not condemned: but he that believeth not is condemned already, because he hath not believed in the name of the only begotten Son of God. – John 3:18

CHAPTER ONE

1:1 The book of the generation of Jesus Christ, the son of David, the son of Abraham.

The book of the generation – that is a fairly common phrase in Jewish writing, meaning the account of the life of the subject named individual, his ancestors, and a few notable descendants. The genealogy of Jesus the Christ is here divided into three classes of fourteen generations each.

Concerning this genealogy of our Savior, observe the chief intention. It is not a needless genealogy. It is not a vain-glorious one, as those of "great men" frequently tend to be. Every family tree has some good and some bad in it. Of what value then are the ancient pedigrees? Some of them are given to show evidence in proving a title or to back up a claim such as this one. This one proves that Jesus is of the nation and of the family out of which The Messiah was to arise. It is, therefore, proof that Jesus is of the lineage of prophecy and promise. The promise of the blessing was to Abraham and his seed. The promise of dominion was to David and his seed. By Him all the families of the earth are to be blessed and ruled. By the setting forth of this genealogy at a time when it could be, and no doubt was, checked against the existing records and challenged, even corrected, if not accurate, therefore the enemies of The Christ, then and now, cannot successfully argue He lacked the necessary lineage.

> 1:2 Abraham begat Isaac; and Isaac begat Jacob; and Jacob begat Judas and his brethren;

This gospel account begins with Abraham because it was written for Jews and Jewish history begins with Abraham. Luke, on the other hand, was writing for Gentiles and therefore goes back to Adam.

> 1:3 And Judas begat Phares and Zara of Tamar; and Phares begat Esrom; and Esrom begat Aram;
> 1:4 And Aram begat Aminadab; and Aminadab begat Naasson; and Naasson begat Salmon;
> 1:5 And Salmon begat Boaz of Rachab; and Boaz begat Obed of Ruth; and Obed begat Jesse;
> 1:6 And Jesse begat David the king; and David the king begat Solomon of her *that had been the wife* of Urias;
> 1:7 And Solomon begat Roboam; and Roboam begat Abia; and Abia begat Asa;
> 1:8 And Asa begat Josaphat; and Josaphat begat Joram; and Joram begat Ozias;
> 1:9 And Ozias begat Joatham; and Joatham begat Achaz; and Achaz begat Ezekias;
> 1:10 And Ezekias begat Manasses; and Manasses begat Amon; and Amon begat Josias;
> 1:11 And Josias begat Jechonias and his brethren, about the time they were carried away to Babylon:
> 1:12 And after they were brought to Babylon, Jechonias begat Salathiel; and Salathiel begat

Zorobabel;
1:13 And Zorobabel begat Abiud; and Abiud begat Eliakim; and Eliakim begat Azor;
1:14 And Azor begat Sadoc; and Sadoc begat Achim; and Achim begat Eliud;
1:15 And Eliud begat Eleazar; and Eleazar begat Matthan; and Matthan begat Jacob;
1:16 And Jacob begat Joseph the husband of Mary, of whom was born Jesus, who is called Christ.

From this it is clear that the genealogy given here is not that of Mary, but of Joseph; nor has this ever been legitimately questioned. And yet it is here studiously proclaimed that Joseph was not the natural, but only the legal father of our Lord. His birth of a virgin was known only to a few; but the acknowledged descent of his legal father from David secured that the legal descent of Jesus Himself from David should never be questioned. Luke's tracing of Mary's genealogy secured the biological descent of Jesus from David.

Who is called [The] Christ – Christ (Greek) = Mashiach (Hebrew) = anointed one. Among the Jews Prophets, Priests, and kings were anointed in order to legitimize their exercise of their respective offices. In the case of Jesus the demonstrative article should never be omitted for He alone is The Anointed One of God.   He is Yeshua [Jeshua] ha Mashiach. Adam Clarke in his commentary on this verse:

> Hence kings were inaugurated by anointing with oil. Two of these offices only exist in all civilized nations, the sacerdotal and regal; and, in some countries, the priest and king are still consecrated by anointing. In the Hebrew language משח mashach signifies to anoint; and

משיח mashiach, the anointed person. But as no man was ever dignified by holding the three offices, so no person ever had the title Mashiach, the anointed one, but Jesus, The Christ. He alone is King of kings, and Lord of lords: the king who governs the universe, and rules in the hearts of his followers; the prophet, to instruct men in the way wherein they should go; and the great high priest, to make atonement for their sins. Hence he is called the Messias, a corruption of the word המשיח ha-mashiach, The anointed One, in Hebrew; which gave birth to ὁ Χριστος ho Christos, which has precisely the same signification in Greek: of him, Melchisedeck, Abraham, Aaron, David, and others, were illustrious types. But none of these had the title of The Messiah, or The Anointed of God. This does, and ever will, belong exclusively to Jesus, The Christ. – Adam Clarke Commentary

1:17 So all the generations from Abraham to David *are* fourteen generations; and from David until the carrying away into Babylon *are* fourteen generations; and from the carrying away into Babylon unto Christ *are* fourteen generations.

1:18 Now the birth of Jesus Christ was on this wise: When as his mother Mary was espoused to Joseph, before they came together, she was found with child of the Holy Ghost.

During the betrothal the woman lived at her father's house while the man made preparations for a house in which they would live and begin to raise their children. This phase of the marriage was quite binding on both sides and a breach of this contract was considered as a case of adultery and it could only be broken by a regular divorce decree. What conversation had taken place between Mary and Joseph we are not informed of, she probably told him all about it as soon as she became actually aware that she was pregnant and revealed it to him not in shame but in reverential awe as she attempted to relate the revelation from God, but the issue was not resolved for him until God sent him assurance that things were as she had said.

> 1:19 Then Joseph her husband, being a just *man,* and not willing to make her a publick example, was minded to put her away privily.

Some imagine that Joseph was at that time a widower and that those who are called the brethren of Jesus (Matt 13:55) were Joseph's children by a former wife, but that is a completely unnecessary construct. Joseph was a just man; she a virtuous woman. There was no requirement for them not to have children following the birth of Jesus and it would, in fact, be a very natural and a to be expected sort of thing that they would.

While Joseph was disappointed by her apparent infidelity he did not act spitefully towards her and he was not willing to take advantage of the law against her if she be guilty. He was a righteous and just man but also inclined towards mercy as God is. In the case of a betrothed damsel, the law charitably supposed that she cried out (Deut 22:26) and she was not to be punished but the guilty man was.

The law of God seeks to put fear into the evil doers while being tempered with mercy for those who were perhaps overtaken in the fault and ought to be restored with the spirit of meekness (properly termed); threatening, even when it is just, must be moderated.

Joseph, we are informed, was thoughtful, unlike Judah in Genesis 38:24 who in a somewhat similar case (on the surface anyway) hastily passed a severe sentence and then afterwards he had to publicly acknowledge his daughter-in-law to be much more righteous and honorable than he. We may also take notice of this; it is the thoughtful, not the unthinking whom God will guide. After the unthinking one makes a mess of things, God may help him pick up the pieces but that is generally only if he becomes thoughtful enough to ask…seek….

> 1:20 But while he thought on these things, behold, the angel of the Lord appeared unto him in a dream, saying, Joseph, thou son of David, fear not to take unto thee Mary thy wife: for that which is conceived in her is of the Holy Ghost.

> 1:21 And she shall bring forth a son, and thou shalt call his name JESUS: for he shall save his people from their sins.

Jesus – Joshua – Yeshua, He saves, delivers. His great errand was to make an atonement for, and to destroy, sin. The perfection of His work is not that it makes an allowance for sin but makes an atonement for it; not that it tolerates sin, which it does not, but that it destroys it. The privilege of every believer in Jesus The Christ is deliverance from all the power, guilt, and pollution of sin. Jesus is the holy one of God the true Messiah, see Acts 2:36; 1st Cor 16:22; 1st John 2:22, 4:15.

Sin is itself the greatest of all miseries. It is commission of treason against God and yourself. It is the source of all other miseries. "Some would rather He [Jesus} had come to save them from poverty, pains, death; not knowing that to save from sins is to save from all these." – J. Bennet, D. D. Nowhere else can we find salvation from sin. Jesus saves His people from the pollution of sin; not in their sin, but from their sins. Jesus does not seek to make us comfortable in sin but freed from sin.

"He shall save his people 'from'," not "in" as too many seem to try to read into the Scripture. The great business of Jesus in the world, His purpose, was to set us free from the bondage; to make an atonement for, and to destroy, sin. Not to make us comfortable in captivity to, but to release the captives of, sin. Deliverance from all the power, guilt, and pollution of sin is the privilege of every genuine believer in The Christ.

> The perfection of the Gospel system is not that it makes allowances for sin, but that it makes an atonement for it: not that it tolerates sin, but that it destroys it. – Adam Clarke

Often the term "Christ" gets confused with the concept of a surname but that is not Jesus' last name, it is a title, the Greek word for "Messiah." Quite frequently we see the name "Jesus" added to the term "Christ" in the New Testament so that not only is Jesus pointed out as the true Savior, but also that He might be pointed out as the true Messiah in opposition to the unbelief of the majority of the Jewish folk in this current age.

This name Jesus," said St. Bernard, "it is honey in the mouth, harmony in the ear, melody in the heart." "This name Jesus," said St. Anselm, "it is a name of comfort to sinners when they call upon Him." "This name of Jesus," said

Christopher Sutton, "it suppleth the hardness of our hearts, it cherisheth the weakness of our faith, enlighteneth the darkness of our soul, and maketh man look with a cheerful countenance towards the throne of grace."

The name "Jesus" was no new name, coined in the courts of heaven, and carried to earth for the first time by the lips of the angel messenger. A new name is cold and meaningless, and stirs no memories of the past. There is warmth about an old familiar name which no new combination of letters can even begin to hope to rival, and so it was an old name, a name with a history behind it, that the angel gave to the unborn Son of Mary. There was more than one little Jewish boy who bore that name at that very time. The ancient historical records revel to us that in the high priest's family alone there were no less than three, each of whom would one day have his turn at being high priest. There was Jesus, son of Sapphia, who would one day become a famous brigand chief, and, still more famous, Jesus surnamed Barabbas. Oh yes, you know Jesus Barabbas because he is that one whom the people would prefer one day over the Jesus called The Christ. Then there was Jesus Justus, who would one day become the trusted helper of St. Paul, and Jesus the father of Elymas, the sorcerer, St. Paul's opponent in Cyprus. There was Jesus the friend of Josephus, and Jesus Thebuti the priest, and Jesus the peasant, whom Josephus the historian tells us about who would one day terrify Jerusalem with his warning cries.

Over many a little living Jesus a mother's head was bending on the day when Mary clasped her new-born baby to her bosom. How came it to be that so many boys were called by the same name? We know what makes a name popular at the present day; it is because that name is borne by the popular hero of the hour. How many girls were christened Florence, after the lady with the lamp! The Boer war produced a practically never-ending crop of little Roberts. And so it has always been. Those Jewish boys were all called Jesus after two great national heroes who had borne that name in the past.

1. Who were those heroes? Where do we find the name "Jesus" in the Old Testament? We do not find it anywhere, nor do we expect to find it; for we are all familiar with the way a name changes as it passes from one language to another—how, for example, the Hebrew Johanan becomes in English John, and in Ireland Shawn, and in German Hans, and in Russian Ivan, and in Spanish Juan, and in Italian Giovanni; the name is the same, but the form varies according to the language. Now the Old Testament and the New Testament were written in different languages. The Old Testament was written in Hebrew, and the New Testament was written in Greek; and thus the same names appear under different forms. Elijah, for example, in the New Testament is always called Elias. And so when we search the Hebrew Old Testament for the Greek name Jesus we would expect to find some change in the spelling.

(1) As a matter of fact we meet the name for the first time in the thirteenth chapter of the Book of Numbers and the sixteenth verse, where we read that "Moses called Hoshea the son of Nun Joshua" (which means "Jehovah is salvation"). Jesus and Joshua are exactly the same name, only one is the Greek form and the other is the Hebrew. Joshua the son of Nun the commander-in-chief of the Lord's people, under whom

they conquered their inheritance, the leader who brought them out of the desert to the land of milk and honey, the captain who led them to victory, though foes were strong and crafty, the ruler who settled every family in the precise position which God appointed for it, and there gave it rest—he is the first who bears the name "Jesus" in the pages of history.

(2) But this Jesus died, and the centuries passed on, and a time came when the people lost the land that had been given them, when for their sins they were carried away captive to Babylon, and then, after forty miserable years, the second Jesus came—Jeshua the high priest, who led the people back to the land that had been lost by sin; Jeshua, who rebuilt the Temple and restored the worship of God; Jeshua, who was crowned with gold by the prophet Zechariah, as the type and forerunner of a greater High Priest who was to come; Jeshua, the son of Jehozadak, was the second Jesus in history.

3. And now we can appreciate something of the associations of the name; we can realize a little of what the message, "Thou shalt call his name Jesus," would mean to a pious Jew like Joseph. Thou shalt name Him after the great captain who drove the Canaanites from the land. Thou shalt name Him after the great high priest who brought back the people out of bondage. Thou shalt call Him Jesus; for He, too, shall be a Saviour. "He shall save his people from their sins."

Man is the principle of the religion of the Neo-Hegelians, and intellect is the climax of man. Their religion, then, is the religion of intellect. There you have the two worlds: Christianity brings and preaches salvation by the conversion of the will,—humanism by the emancipation of the mind. One attacks the heart, the other the brain. Both wish to enable man to reach his ideal. But the ideal suffers, if not by its content, at least by the disposition of its content, by the predominance and sovereignty given to this or that inner power. For one, the mind is the organ of the soul; for the other, the soul is an inferior state of the mind; the one wishes to enlighten by making better, the other to make better by enlightening. It is the difference between Socrates and Jesus. *The cardinal question is that of sin.* The question of immanence or of dualism is secondary. The Trinity, the life to come, paradise and hell, may cease to be dogmas and spiritual realities, the form and the letter may vanish away,—the question of humanity remains: What is it which saves? – Amiel's Journal (translated by Mrs. Humphry Ward, British Novelist in 1884)

1:22 Now all this was done, that it might be fulfilled which was spoken of the Lord by the prophet, saying,

1:23 Behold, a virgin shall be with child, and shall bring forth a son, and they shall call his name Emmanuel, which being interpreted is, God with us.

Isaiah 7:14

They – all His people, Jew and Gentile, those who call Him "Master," "Savior," and "Lord," they are they who shall call Him, shall acknowledge Him to be, The "Emmanuel."

Both the Divine and human nature of our Lord, as well as the miraculous conception, appear to be pointed out in the prophecy quoted here by the evangelist: - He shall be called עמנו־אל IM-MENU-EL; literally, The Strong God with Us: similar to those words in the New Testament: - The Word which was God - was made flesh, and dwelt among us, full of grace and truth: John 1:1, John 1:14. And, God was manifested in the flesh: 1Ti 3:16. So that we are to understand, God with us, to imply God incarnated - God in human nature. This seems farther evident from the words of the prophet, Isa 7:15. Butter and honey shall he eat - he shall be truly man, grow up and be nourished in a human, natural way; which refers to his being With Us, i.e. incarnated. To which the prophet adds, That he may know to refuse the evil and choose the good: - or rather, According to his knowledge, לדעתו le-daato, reprobating the evil, and choosing the good. This refers to him as God; and is the same idea given by this prophet, Isa 53:11 : By (or in) his knowledge (the knowledge of Christ crucified, בדעתו be-daato) shall my righteous servant sanctify many; for he shall bear their offenses. Now this union of the Divine and human nature is termed a sign or miracle, אות oth, i.e. something which exceeds the power of nature to produce. And this miraculous union was to be brought about in a miraculous way: Behold a Virgin shall conceive: the word is very emphatic, העלמה ha-almah, The virgin; the only one that ever was, or ever shall be, a mother in this way. But the Jews, and some called Christians, who have espoused their desperate cause, assert, that "the word עלמה almah does not signify a Virgin only; for it is applied, Pro 30:19, to signify a young married woman." I answer, that this latter text is no proof of the contrary doctrine: the words דרך גבר בעלמה derec geber be-almah, the way of a man with a maid, cannot be proved to mean that for which it is produced: beside, one of De Rossi's MSS. reads בעלמיו be-almaiu, the way of a strong, or stout, man (גבר geber) In His Youth; and in this reading the Syriac, Septuagint, Vulgate, and Arabic agree, which are followed by the first version in the English language, as it stands in a MS. in my own possession - *the weie of a man in his waring youthe*; so that this place, the only one that can with any probability of success be produced, were the interpretation contended for correct, which I am by no means disposed to admit, proves nothing. Beside, the consent of so many versions in the opposite meaning deprives it of much of its influence in this question.

The word עלמה almah, comes from עלם alam, to lie hid, be concealed; and we are told that "virgins were so called, because they were concealed or closely kept up in their fathers' houses, till the time of their marriage." This is not correct: see the case of Rebecca, Gen 24:43 (note), and my note there: that of Rachel, Gen 29:6, Gen 29:9, and the note there also: and see the case of Miriam, the sister of Moses, Exo 2:8, and also the Chaldee paraphrase on Lam 1:4, where the virgins are represented as going out in the dance. And see also the whole history of Ruth. This being concealed, or kept at home, on which so much stress is laid, is purely fanciful; for we find that young unmarried women drew water, kept sheep, gleaned publicly in the fields, etc., etc., and the same works they perform among the Turcomans to the present day. This reason, therefore, does not account for the radical meaning of the word; and we must seek it elsewhere. Another well known and often used root in the Hebrew tongue will cast light on this subject. This is גלה galah, which signifies to reveal, make manifest, or uncover, and is often applied to matrimonial connections, in different parts of the Mosaic law: עלם alam, therefore, may be considered as implying the concealment of the virgin, as such, till lawful marriage had taken place. **A virgin was not called עלמה almah, because she was concealed by being kept at home in her father's house, which is not true, but literally and physically, because, as a woman, she had not been uncovered - she had not known man. This fully applies to the blessed virgin**: see Luke 1:34. "How can this be, seeing I know no man?" and this text throws much light on the subject before us. This also is in perfect agreement with the ancient prophecy, "The seed of the woman shall bruise the head of the serpent," Gen 3:15; for the person who was to destroy the work of the devil was to be **the progeny of the woman, without any concurrence of the man**. And, hence, the text in Genesis speaks as fully of the virgin state of the person, from whom Christ, according to the flesh, should come, as that in the prophet, or this in the evangelist. According to the original promise, there was to be a seed, a human being, who should destroy sin; but **this seed or human being must come from the woman Alone; and no woman Alone, could produce such a human being, without being a virgin**. Hence, A virgin shall bear a son, is the very spirit and meaning of the original text, independently of the illustration given by the prophet; and the fact recorded by the evangelist is the proof of the whole. But how could that be a sign to Ahaz, which was to take place so many hundreds of years after? I answer, **the meaning of the prophet is plain: not only Rezin and Pekah should be unsuccessful against Jerusalem at that time, which was the fact;**

but Jerusalem, Judea, and the house of David, should be both preserved, notwithstanding their depressed state, and the multitude of their adversaries, **till the time should come when a Virgin should bear a son. This is a most remarkable circumstance - the house of David could never fail, till a virgin should conceive and bear a son - nor did it: but when that incredible and miraculous fact did take place, the kingdom and house of David became extinct**! This is an irrefragable confutation of every argument a Jew can offer in vindication of his opposition to the Gospel of Christ. Either the prophecy in Isaiah has been fulfilled, or the kingdom and house of David are yet standing. But the kingdom of David, we know, is destroyed: and where is the man, Jew or Gentile, that can show us a single descendant of David on the face of the earth? The prophecy could not fail - the kingdom and house of David have failed; the virgin, therefore, must have brought forth her son - and this son is Jesus, the Christ. Thus Moses, Isaiah, and Matthew concur; and facts, the most unequivocal, have confirmed the whole! Behold the wisdom and providence of God!

Notwithstanding what has been said above, it may be asked, In what sense could this name Immanuel be applied to Jesus Christ, if he be not truly and properly God? Could the Spirit of truth ever design that Christians should receive him as an angel or a mere man, and yet, in the very beginning of the Gospel history, apply a character to him which belongs only to the most high God? Surely no. In what sense, then, is Christ God With Us? Jesus is called Immanuel, or God with us, in his incarnation. - God united to our nature - God with man - God in man. - God with us, by his continual protection. - God with us, by the influences of his Holy Spirit - in the holy sacrament - in the preaching of his word - in private prayer. And God with us, through every action of our life, that we begin, continue, and end in his name. He is God with us, to comfort, enlighten, protect, and defend us in every time of temptation and trial, in the hour of death, in the day of judgment; and God with us, and in us, and we with and in him, to all eternity. – Adam Clarke, emphasis mine.

Perhaps you, dear reader, will say, "Pastor, why did you include this lengthy quote from Dr. Clarke?" My purpose, is to show that over 200 years ago the critics were answered quite clearly and quite definitively, and they pose no new, intelligent, objections to the Gospel record. If anything, their objections are even more foolish now than they were then because in their own foolishness they are trying to act wiser than those of us who choose to believe God. Therefore, Romans 1:22, 28 applies to them.

The virginity of Mary prior to the birth of Jesus The Christ is an article of utmost consequence to the Christian system, therefore an article of faith: the idea of her perpetual virginity, on the other hand, is of no beneficial consequence. If there were a midwife present at the Birth and assisting .... Can you imagine the wide-eyed wonder of Mabel the Midwife, who has delivered dozens and dozens of babies stuttering and stammering "A virgin, a virgin has given birth, how can it be?"

> 1:24 Then Joseph being raised from sleep did as the angel of the Lord had bidden him, and took unto him his wife:

Joseph's obedience to the divine directive was no doubt

done without delay. Although it was contrary to his former sentiments and intention he quickly, without delay, obeyed the heavenly vision for delay in obeying a divine directive following confirmation of its authenticity invites doubt and quickly degenerates into disobedience. It would be in deep and reverential joy that he would now take his espoused wife unto his care and comfort her who had been logically albeit unjustly under suspicion.

Christ was first-born and thus he would be called whether or not his mother had any children after Him. There is no scriptural proof that she and Joseph had no further children, rather the Greek word employed here strongly indicates that she did, in fact, have other children after Jesus. There is another word that denotes one and only as in: "the only begotten Son of God" as per John 3:16.

Jesus' mission was not to save his people from foreign domination but to save them from sin.

> 1:25 And knew her not till she had brought forth her firstborn son: and he called his name JESUS.

> This name was given by the command of God and declared when eight days old when, according to Jewish law, he was circumcised: thus He had the name Savior given when He first began to shed that blood without which there can be no remission of sins.

CHAPTER TWO

2:1 Now when Jesus was born in Bethlehem of Judaea in the days of Herod the king, behold, there came wise men from the east to Jerusalem,

Bethlehem, Hebrew, House of Bread. The birthplace of Him who calls Himself the Bread of Life (John 6:35)

Wise men, Magi. Wycliffe translates as Kings. It was a priestly caste among the Medes and Persian. Daniel became leader of such an order in Babylon – Daniel 2:48. Which also helps explain why the Noah's flood story influenced the Gilgamesh epic, not the other way round, which fact many archeologists tend to overlook.

2:2 Saying, Where is he that is born King of the Jews? For we have seen his star in the east, and are come to worship him.

All through the ages this incident has been glorified and magnified by pen and song. The Epiphany is one thing for which Matthew makes no claim of a fulfillment of prophecy but perhaps Psalm 72:10-15 spoke of it.

In the second century and since that time others have decided to embellish the story in various ways. Some have even tried to give them names and attempted to add further "details" to the legendary folklore. Most, unfortunately, seem to completely miss the important, but simple, details provided in Matthew's brief narrative as they try to focus on what we are not told.

What sort of star was it which they tell us about which started them on their journey? We can be fairly certain that it was not a planet nor a conjunction of planets as Kepler had suggested because the planets were malign to the Magi. It seems far more natural to think of a Nova, one of those sudden apparitions that tell us of a stupendous outburst in the depths of space, bringing to our eyes a new star that in a few weeks or months fades away from sight. There was a Nova in the constellation of Perseus in Feb 1901 which was bright enough to be counted among the first magnitude of stars. Of course, there have been many others; the Magi's star did not have to be as bright as the 1901 one in order to gain their attention. Professional astronomers would notice a new star which would go unnoticed by those who paid little, if any attention to the night sky. Whatever it was, its position counted more for them than its brilliance. They had some knowledge of the Jewish Messianic hopes. Daniel had been a prominent member of their community and there were probably still some Jews living in their country.

In the QUARTELY JOURNAL OF THE ROYAL ASTRONOMICAL SOCIETY 18 (1977), pp 443-449 three astronomers identified it as a nova which Chinese astronomers observed for 70 days in 5/4 BC. Another document citing it, F. Munter, Der Stern Der Weisen (1827), p 29.

From Daniel they would have known the time was drawing near for his prophecy to be fulfilled. Daniel's "book" could have been one of those that had sat neglected, but safely stored away in their library, for many years but then the Spirit of God moved one of their number to read it and piqued their interest and caused them to calculate approximately when it could come to completion. Therefore their hearts and minds were fully prepared when the Nova, or whatever it was, was revealed to them.

Some have also suggested that the Magi were descendants of Abraham's wife Ketura. Centuries after their visit one of them turns black and then their skulls are "discovered" in Cologne in the twelfth century. The twelfth century produced a plethora of pretend artifacts. Some have suggested that the Magi were descendants of Noah's sons Shem, Ham, and Japhet. The fact of the matter remains that apart from the very limited information provided by the Scripture we know nothing, absolutely nothing, of the Magi and we really don't need to know anything further about them than what Scripture has revealed. Realistically, ladies and gentlemen, have we actually learned all that God wanted us to learn from His Scripture? Until we reach that point there is no need for us to be majoring in the minor stuff.

"Wise men - The first fruits of the Gentiles. Probably they were Gentile philosophers, who, through the Divine assistance, had improved their knowledge of nature, as a means of leading to the knowledge of the one true God. Nor is it unreasonable to suppose, that God had favoured them with some extraordinary revelations of himself, as he did Melchisedec, Job, and several others, who were not of the family of Abraham; to which he never intended absolutely to confine his favours. The title given them in the original was anciently given to all philosophers, or men of learning; those particularly who were curious in examining the works of nature, and observing the motions of the heavenly bodies. From the east - So Arabia is frequently called in Scripture. It lay to the east of Judea, and was famous for gold, frankincense, and myrrh. We have seen his star - Undoubtedly they had before heard Balaam's prophecy. And probably when they saw this unusual star, it was revealed to them that this prophecy was fulfilled. In the east - That is, while we were in the east." – John Wesley's Explanatory Notes

There is a light which comes only to those who seek in the night, and can feel after what they cannot find, and can still nurse "the unconquerable hope," and never lose heart. There is a light which is always just ahead of where you stand. You must follow if you would arrive, and the following must never cease. God never lacks the means to guide earnest inquirers.

2:3 When Herod the king had heard *these things,* he was troubled, and all Jerusalem with him.

Herod was an Edomite who only held the title "King of the Jews" by Roman appointment. In his early years he had been good and had done some very good and notable deeds but now he was plagued by paranoia and had become quite evil. God Himself warns us in Ezekiel 33:13,18 that when a righteous person forsakes his righteousness and does evil all his righteousness will be forgotten; that works in heaven the same as on earth.

"As the Magi seek a redeemer, so Herod fears a

successor. If His birth makes proud Kings tremble, what will his tribunal as a Judge do?" – St Augustine

Herod's agitation was probably occasioned by the agreement of the account of the magi, with an opinion predominant throughout the east at that time, and particularly in Judea, that some great person would soon make his appearance and take upon himself the universal empire that would be beneficial to all his subjects. It was that belief that stopped the Romans from doing the forced-assimilation which they routinely did to many other people groups which they had conquered.

The Roman historian Seutonius said, "An ancient and settled persuasion prevailed throughout the east, that the fates had decreed some to proceed from Judea, who should attain universal empire. Tacitus said, "Many were persuaded, that it was contained in the ancient books of their priests, that at about that very time the east should prevail: and that some should proceed from Judea and possess the dominion." For that reason the Jewish people were given a level of autonomy not granted to other conquered peoples. However by the time 69 AD had rolled around the Roman leadership had not seen the great one emerge and some began to promote the idea that Vespasian and Titus were possibly the fulfillment of the ancient prophecies and therefore, because the Jews had apparently failed to produce the King of Kings, it was time to be rid of that pesky, ungrateful, and rebellious Jewish nation.

From the Roman perspective, the Jewish people had a lot that they should have been grateful for: Relative peace and safety; the freedom to build their magnificent temple; their ability to remain as a separate people group within the Roman Empire.

2:4 And when he had gathered all the chief priests and scribes of the people together, he demanded of them where Christ should be born.

2:5 And they said unto him, In Bethlehem of Judaea: for thus it is written by the prophet,

Herod demands to know where The Messiah was to be born – the Priests do the research and give an answer but it appears they were so dead spiritually that they did not even think to go and see if it was now happening as foretold. Supposedly they were looking forward to the arrival of their promised deliverer but their actions demonstrated they were more interested in maintaining their positions of power.

2:6 And thou Bethlehem, *in* the land of Judah, art not the least among the princes of Judah: for out of thee shall come a Governor, that shall rule my people Israel.

2:7 Then Herod, when he had privily called the wise men, enquired of them diligently what time the star appeared.

2:8 And he sent them to Bethlehem, and said, Go and search diligently for the young child; and when ye have found *him,* bring me word again, that I may come and worship him also.

2:9 When they had heard the king, they departed; and, lo, the star, which they saw in the east, went before them, till it came and stood over where the young child was.

The star led the wise men to Bethlehem and "stood over the place where the young child was." Not the stable, but the house into which Mary and Joseph had moved, possibly only a few days following the birth of Jesus. Exactly how long after Messiah's birth it was before the wise men arrived we do not know, tradition says twelve days; hence twelve days of Christmas, but it may have been months. Mary may have told Matthew but God may have told him to leave that information out because it was not important or Matthew himself may have accurately considered it unimportant. The important part is that the pilgrims entered, paid proper homage, and were satisfied that they had found the one they diligently sought.

> 2:10 When they saw the star, they rejoiced with exceeding great joy.
>
> 2:11 And when they were come into the house, they saw the young child with Mary his mother, and fell down, and worshipped him: and when they had opened their treasures, they presented unto him gifts; gold, and frankincense, and myrrh.
>
> 2:12 And being warned of God in a dream that they should not return to Herod, they departed into their own country another way.

Before the Russian Revolution in 1917 the Russian children received Christmas gifts on the 12th day of Christmas, Epiphany. After the revolution the government discouraged and suppressed tales with religious connotations. After the fall of the Soviet Union old beliefs began to return. Among them is that an old woman, the Baboushka, was at work in her house when the wise men from the East passed by on their way to find and pay homage to the Christ Child. "Come with us," they said, "we have seen His star in the East, and we go to worship Him." "I will come, but not now," she answered; "I have my house to set in order; when that is done, I will follow, and find Him." But when her work was done, the three kings had already continued on their way across the desert, and the star was no longer visible in the darkened heavens. She hurried along in haste to try to catch up with them but she never found them or the Christ Child for she had neglected her opportunity for divine guidance, but she is living, according to the tradition, and searching for Him still. For His sake, she takes care of all His children. It is she, they say, who in Russian homes fills the stockings and dresses the tree on Christmas morn. The children are awakened with the cry, "Behold the Baboushka," and springing up, they hope to see her before she vanishes out of the window. She fancies, so the tradition goes, that in each poor little one whom she warms and feeds, she may find and honor the Christ Child whom she neglected ages ago.

> 2:13 And when they were departed, behold, the angel of the Lord appeareth to Joseph in a dream, saying, Arise, and take the young child and his mother, and flee into Egypt, and be thou there until I bring thee word: for Herod will seek the young child to destroy him.

Flee into Egypt - Many Jews had settled in Egypt; not only those who had fled thither in the time of Jeremiah, see Jeremiah 48; but many others who had settled there also, on account of the temple which Onias IV. had built at Heliopolis. Those who could speak the Greek tongue enjoyed many advantages in that country: besides, they had the Greek version of the Septuagint, which had been translated nearly 300 years before this time. Egypt was now a Roman province, and the rage of Herod could not pursue the holy family to this place. There is an apocryphal work in Arabic, called the Gospel of the infancy, which pretends to relate all the acts of Jesus and Mary while in Egypt. I have taken the pains to read this through, and have found it to be a piece of gross superstition, having nothing to entitle it to a shadow of credibility. – Adam Clarke (about 1800)

2:14 When he arose, he took the young child and his mother by night, and departed into Egypt:

2:15 And was there until the death of Herod: that it might be fulfilled which was spoken of the Lord by the prophet, saying, Out of Egypt have I called my son.

2:16 Then Herod, when he saw that he was mocked of the wise men, was exceeding wroth, and sent forth, and slew all the children that were in Bethlehem, and in all the coasts thereof, from two years old and under, according to the time which he had diligently enquired of the wise men.

Herod, the king of the Jews through Roman favor, represents the foolish hostility of Jew and Gentile to The Christ of God; that hostility produces, time and again, great human distress. Herod did not disbelieve the star or the prophecies interpreted by the priests and scribes and therefore we can see he was fighting against the one true God, the God of father Abraham, Isaac, and Jacob. Herod is an example of the infatuating influences of sin and its power to prevent the proper conclusions a rational being should be able to make. He thought, in his sin darkened mind, he could prevent the prophecies from being fulfilled. The massacre of the infant children at Bethlehem was just one of the prophecies he inadvertently fulfilled in opposing the will of God.

Herod, failing to discover the Messiah by stealth, sought to destroy Him by indiscriminate cruelty. Egypt was the nearest of Roman provinces independent of Herod's influence and convenient for a return at the proper time.

2:17 Then was fulfilled that which was spoken by Jeremy the prophet, saying,

Jeremiah 31:15

2:18 In Rama was there a voice heard, lamentation, and weeping, and great mourning, Rachel weeping *for* her children, and would not be comforted, because they are not.

These words, as they stand in Jeremiah, undoubtedly relate to the Babylonish captivity. Rachel, the mother of Joseph and Benjamin, was buried in the neighborhood of Bethlehem (Gen 35:19), where her sepulchre is still shown. She is figuratively represented as rising from the tomb and uttering a double lament for the loss of her children - first, by a bitter captivity, and now by a bloody death. And a foul deed it was. O ye mothers of Bethlehem! methinks I hear you asking why your innocent babes should be the ram caught in the thicket, while Isaac escapes. I cannot tell you, but one thing I know, that ye shall, some of you, live to see a day when that Babe of Bethlehem shall be Himself the Ram, caught in another sort of thicket, in order that your babes may escape a worse doom than they now endure. And if these babes of yours be now in glory, through the dear might of that blessed Babe, will they not deem it their honor that the tyrant's rage was exhausted upon themselves instead of their infant Lord? – Jamieson, Fausset, and Brown Commentary

Herod imagined that he had prevented or at least postponed the Old Testament prophecies, but whatever craftiness or cruel campaigns are created in corrupted human hearts the counsels of the Lord shall stand and succeed.

> 2:19 But when Herod was dead, behold, an angel of the Lord appeareth in a dream to Joseph in Egypt,

This did not take place very long after the flight to Egypt as we are able to deduce from the details provided by Josephus in *Antiquities*.

> 2:20 Saying, Arise, and take the young child and his mother, and go into the land of Israel: for they are dead which sought the young child's life.

> 2:21 And he arose, and took the young child and his mother, and came into the land of Israel.

> 2:22 But when he heard that Archelaus did reign in Judaea in the room of his father Herod, he was afraid to go thither: notwithstanding, being warned of God in a dream, he turned aside into the parts of Galilee:

Augustus refused to grant Archelaus the title of king until such time as he had proven himself, which he failed to do; therefore he never attained the title but did succeed in getting himself banished after about ten years when the people had repeatedly appealed to Caesar for his removal. The scepter had apparently "departed" from Judah but the prophecy of promised Messiah had already been fulfilled although most failed to see.

> 2:23 And he came and dwelt in a city called Nazareth:

that it might be fulfilled which was spoken by the prophets, He shall be called a Nazarene.

CHAPTER THREE

3:1 In those days came John the Baptist, preaching in the wilderness of Judaea,

> **Came - preaching -** Κηρυσσων, proclaiming, as a herald, a matter of great and solemn importance to men; the subject not his own, nor of himself, but from that God from whom alone he had received his commission. ... Rosenmuller says, "The verb κηρυσσειν is applied to those who, in the streets, fields, and open air, lift up their voice, that they may be heard by many, and proclaim what has been committed to them by regal or public authority; as the Kerukes among the Greeks, and the Precones among the Romans." – Adam Clarke

Wilderness – Now this had nothing to do with living a hermit's life; his was a transitional ministry between the Mosaic and Christian dispensation/system. It is true that in solitude there are fewer occasions of vice but, let us not forget, there are also fewer opportunities for virtues to be exercised.

It is good to withdraw in order to recharge and reinvigorate oneself occasionally but in order to be salt and light as we are called to be, and make disciples; one has to interact with the world. Solitude is sometimes somewhat conducive to usefulness but solitude for solitude's sake and/or avoiding all interaction with sinners is simply a selfish sham.

Growing up as the son of a priest John may have had more than his fill of the corruption in some of those he saw in the Temple and he withdrew from them to become an Essene but he complied with the call from God to be a change agent.

3:2 And saying, Repent ye: for the kingdom of heaven is at hand.

Repent - Μετανοεω. This was the prime objective of his preaching. The verb μετανοεω is either compounded of μετα, *after*, and νοειν *perceive with the mind, to understand*, which signifies that, after hearing such preaching, the sinner is led to comprehend, that the way he was walking in is the way of misery, death, and hell. The word may also be compounded from μετα *after*, and ανοια, *folly/madness*, which intimates that the whole life of a sinner is nothing better than a continual course of madness and folly: and if one chooses to live in a state of constant opposition to all the dictates of true wisdom; to wage war against his own best interests in time and eternity; to provoke and insult the living God; and, by habitual sin, to prepare himself only for the state of utter misery, by evidences of insanity, which every sinner exhibits plentifully, he thereby accrues the legitimate consequences of his choices. It was from this notion of the word, that the Latin writers termed repentance: *resipiscentia*, a growing sentient, or growing wise again, from *re* and *sapere*; or, as Tertullian has it, "*Resipiscentia, quasi receptio mentis ad se,*" restoring the mind to itself: Contra Marcion, lib. ii.

Repentance, then, would imply that a measure of Divine wisdom has been communicated to the sinner, and that he thereby becomes wise, or enlightened, unto salvation. Therefore his mind, his purposes, his opinions, and his inclinations, are changed; and that, in consequence, there is a total change in his conduct. It need scarcely be remarked, that, in this state, a person feels a deep anguish of soul, because he now recognizes that he has sinned against God, unfitted himself for heaven, and exposed his soul to hell. True penitents have other thoughts of God and The Christ, sin and holiness, of this world and the other, than the unrepentant ones. Hence, a true penitent has that sorrow, whereby he forsakes sin, not only because it has been ruinous to his own soul, but because he finally comprehends it has been offensive to God. Sinning daily in thought, word, and deed is no longer an acceptable option; the pursuit of holiness becomes paramount.

> 3:3 For this is he that was spoken of by the prophet Esaias, saying, The voice of one crying in the wilderness, Prepare ye the way of the Lord, make his paths straight.

> Isaiah 40:3. - "John was Christ's forerunner, as the ploughman goes before the sower. Before good work can be expected, there must be excitement. The turf-bound surface of communities must be torn up, the compacted soil turned to the air and light. Upon the rough furrows, and not on the shorn lawn, is there hope for the seed." – *H. W. Beecher*

Thirty years have passed since "all Jerusalem was troubled" by the rumor of The Messiah's birth. Nothing more had been heard of Him since, except for maybe a minor stir about twelve years following that rumor. There have been several political changes, mostly for the worse. Pontius Pilate has just entered into his office and he doesn't like the turn his career path has just made with this dead-end assignment. He is now making some mistakes and sowing some seeds he is really going to regret.

"...Prepare ye the way...":

The idea is taken from the practice of eastern monarchs, who, whenever they entered upon an expedition, or took a journey through a desert country, sent harbingers before them, to prepare all things for their passage; and pioneers to open the passes, to level the ways, and to remove all impediments. The officers appointed to superintend such preparations were called by the Latins, *stratores*.

Diodorus's account of the march of Semiramis into Media and Persia, will give us a clear notion of the preparation of the way for a royal expedition.

"In her march to Ecbatane, she came to the Zarcean mountain, which, extending many furlongs, and being full of craggy precipices and deep hollows, could not be passed without making a great compass about. Being therefore desirous of leaving an everlasting memorial of herself, as well as shortening the way, she ordered the precipices to be digged down, and the hollows to be filled up; and, at a great expense, she made a shorter and more expeditious road, which, to this day, is called from her, The road of Semiramis. Afterwards she went into Persia, and all the other countries of Asia, subject to her dominion; and, wherever she went, she ordered the mountains and precipices to be leveled, raised causeways in the plain country, and, at a great expense, made the ways passable." Diod. Sic. lib. ii. and Bp. Lowth.

The Jewish Church was that desert country, to which John was sent, to announce the coming of the Messiah. It was destitute at that time of all religious cultivation, and of the spirit and practice of piety; and John was sent to prepare the way of the Lord, by preaching the doctrine of repentance. The desert is therefore to be considered as affording a proper emblem of the rude state of the Jewish Church, which is the true wilderness meant by the prophet, and in which John was to prepare the way of the promised Messiah. – Adam Clarke

3:4 And the same John had his raiment of camel's hair, and a leathern girdle about his loins; and his meat was locusts and wild honey.

Some commentators, probably because their palates were not oriented that way, are of the opinion that this must refer to the top of a certain plant but others point out that the insect called the locust is still an article of food in some Asiatic countries. John's simple diet and clothes stood in stark contrast to the Scribes and Pharisees who ran in the posh political circles of Jerusalem.

3:5 Then went out to him Jerusalem, and all Judaea, and all the region round about Jordan,

From the metropolitan center to the surrounding environs, folks were flocking to see and hear John. It is mostly out of curiosity that they come

3:6 And were baptized of him in Jordan, confessing their sins.

Confessing their sins – Confessing of sin should not be made to just every one we meet; it should be discriminating.

1. It should be honest.
2. The moment a man attempts to be honest with himself in respect to his moral character, and to make confession before God, everything that is in him rises up against him.
   a. Reason. Reason suborned by his feelings refuses to investigate. It returns false reports, i.e. "I'm not so bad as others."
   b. Pride. The mouth of pride has the lockjaw, when it is a question of confessing wrongs committed.
   c. Vanity. Vanity teaches men to have greater regard for the opinions of men rather than God.
   d. Conscience. Conscience tends to stop the one ready to confess by saying "Stop, insincere hypocrite...."
   e. Pruudence. "Leave well enough alone." The past is passed, just leave it alone; but, the fact of the matter is, it won't leave you alone.

Why confess? Here is an illustration regarding an earthen dam that may help:

Ah! The bank is breaking away. A craw-fish has pierced it. The stream is working, and working and working. The engineer is sent up to see if all is safe. He sees that a stream is running through the bank, big as his finger. He looks at it, and waits to see if the stream enlarges. Soon it is as big as his two fingers. He waits a little longer, and it is as big as his hand. It is wearing on either side the opening, and the waters are beginning to find it out, and slowly they swirl on the inside towards this point. It will not be many hours before the bank will be so torn that it will give way, and the flood will pour through the *crevasse*. But the engineer goes back and says, "Well, there was a little rill there. But it was a very beautiful place: I never saw a prettier bank than that. The trees that grow in the neighborhood are superb; and the shrubbery there is very fragrant and charming; and the moisture which finds its way through the bank seems to nourish all vegetation near it." "Well, but the *break!* How about that?" "It was something of a break; but, as I was saying, it is a beautiful spot. And right there is a fine plantation; and the man that owns it-" "But how about the *crevasse?* Yes, there was a little *crevasse;* but, as I was saying, all things conspire to make it a lovely scene." What kind of a report is that, of an engineer sent out to investigate, when it is question of impending ruin?

What kind of a report is that, when the elements are at work which will soon launch desolation on the neighborhood? Send the engineer Reason into a man's soul, and ask it to report concerning the habit of drinking in the man. It comes back and says, "Oh! well, he takes a little for the oft infirmities of his stomach; but he is a good fellow, he is a strong man, and his heart is in the right place." "But what about his *habit?* ... He takes a little now and then; but, as I was saying, he is a generous fellow. If you had heard of his kindnesses to that family when they were in distress-" "But what about his *habit?*" – H. W. Beecher.

Baptism – Dunked, poured, or sprinkled? Although much ink has been spilled over whether one mode has greater legitimacy than the others, it is the thing signified, not the mode, which is the essential part of the sacrament. The archeologist's spade has revealed to us that John used more than one mode to accomplish the external part of the sacrament which is absolutely worthless if not accompanied by the necessary internal portion which includes repentance from sin.

Baptism is:

1. An initiatory rite
2. A representative Ordinance
3. A confirmatory rite
4. Not salvific. "Sorry Charlie," Jesus saves, not baptism.

3:7 But when he saw many of the Pharisees and Sadducees come to his baptism, he said unto them, O generation of vipers, who hath warned you to flee from the wrath to come?

To flee – John had strong reason to suspect it was not so much their own spiritual anxieties as it was the popularity of his movement and jealousy that had drawn them out to see what he was up to.

The Pharisees started out as the holiness of heart and life sect, separating themselves from the pollution which had crept into the Jewish national worship system at the time of their formation, but over time they had failed to maintain their purity and had become legalistic and prideful of their outward purity while their personal purity had practically evaporated.

The Sadducees denied the existence of angels and spirits

as well as the resurrection of the dead. They were the Deists of the Jewish nation and very materialistic.

John was probably very much aware that he was sent "In the spirit and power of Elijah," for that is what his father had been told by the angel; but he also knew that was not what they meant by their caustic challenge. They were asking "Are you Elijah risen from the dead?" Of course, he denies that, but he doesn't offer them much of an explanation because he is well aware that they aren't really interested in knowing the truth. He is not going to offer "pearls" to those who would not recognize their value and would only seek other ways to attack rather than accept his message.

As sinners we are exposed to wrath. Wrath against sin is required by Divine holiness. There are many revelations of the wrath of God and declarations in Scripture, i.e. Psalm 7:11; Romans 1:18. As we behold the cross we see the clearest and most awful evidence of the one true God's determination to punish sin and yet to set up the manner whereby pardon may be proffered. Ecclesiastes 12:14; 2nd Thess 1:7-9; 2nd Peter 3:7; Rev 20:11-12, 15.

Is it really so surprising that we should be exhorted to escape? If we perish, it will be made so much the worse by reason of the rejected abundant provisions made for our escape. If we wish to flee from the wrath we must:

1. Hear the voice of warning
2. Flee to Christ, the only refuge – not from.
3. Be in earnest. Keep close to the place of shelter

This wrath is:

1. Divine
2. Deserved

3. Undiluted
4. Accumulated
5. Eternal

3:8 Bring forth therefore fruits meet for repentance:

Repentance is of two sorts; that which is termed legal, and that which is styled evangelical repentance. The former (which is the same that is spoken of here) is a thorough conviction of sin. The latter is a change of heart (and consequently of life) from all sin to all holiness. – John Wesley

Thomas Olivers was an itinerant cobbler, who spent his time working, carousing, and contracting debts. He congratulated himself on his skill in defrauding his creditors. This reprobate Welshman was at last rescued by Methodism, and became one of Mr. John Wesley's itinerant corps. So great had been his wickedness, that his friends thought he must have had some terrible fright, His uncle said to him, "Thou hast been so wicked, thou hast seen the devil." His conscience was awakened. Of his old debts he said, "I feel as great sorrow and confusion as if I had stolen every sum I owed." He resolved to pay the last cent from money due to him from the estate of one of his kindred. With part of his money, he bought a horse, and started on his memorable journey from town to town, preaching Christ, and paying his debts. He went to Whithurst to pay a sixpence. Before his strange pilgrimage was ended, he paid about seventy debts, and had to sell his horse, saddle, and bridle, to finish his payments. Such fruits of repentance were followed by great religious prosperity and usefulness. – *Anon.*

Morality may keep you out of jail, but it takes the blood of Jesus to keep you out of hell. – C. H. Spurgeon

3:9 And think not to say within yourselves, We have Abraham to *our* father: for I say unto you, that God is able of these stones to raise up children unto Abraham.

3:10 And now also the axe is laid unto the root of the trees: therefore every tree which bringeth not forth good fruit is hewn down, and cast into the fire.

Repentance is of two sorts; that which is termed legal, and that which is styled evangelical repentance. The former (which is the same that is spoken of here) is a thorough conviction of sin. The latter is a change of heart (and consequently of life) from all sin to all holiness. – John Wesley

Hear a story, or a parable: In a delightful bit of country, early one summer morning, I walked out to be refreshed by the pure sweet air, the sight of fields and woods, grasses and flowers, beasts and birds, when, presently, I came upon an orchard, into which I entered. The trees were beautiful to behold, the air was fragrant, and fruit was abundant. I wandered on almost enchanted, until, to my great wonder, I came upon a tree having neither bloom nor fruit. I was so painfully impressed that, without any thought of hurting or giving offence, and as to myself, I said, "You poor, lost tree, what can you be doing here? I marvel you are not removed." Upon which, to my astonishment, this tree replied, not without tartness, "Oh, indeed, sir; indeed! No doubt you think you are wise, wise above your fathers. -You think you know much about things, I dare say, but you are in a great mistake. I am neither poor nor lost." "Well," I said, "you have neither leaves nor fruit, and, I should judge, no sap." "What has that to do with it?" it broke out. "Your ignorance is inexcusable. You seem not to know that a great Savior of trees has been down here, and I have believed His gospel, and am saved by grace. I have accepted salvation as a free gift, and, though I have neither leaves nor fruit, I am saved all the same." I looked at it with pity and said, "You are a poor deluded tree; you are not saved at all. You are only a dead, good-for-nothing tree, despite all your talk about grace and redemption. The only salvation you can ever know is to be made living and fruit-bearing. Life, that is salvation. When I come and see you laden with fruit, or even showing signs of leaves, I shall say, ' Ah! that poor tree is saved at last; it has received the gospel and is saved by grace.' " As I turned away, I heard it saying, "You are not sound; you do not understand the gospel." And I thought, so it is, as with trees so with men; they talk as if grace and salvation were something God keeps for them outside themselves, and will not understand nor believe that he who is saved, he who takes Christ fully, and rests on His atoning work alone, "is made free from sin," and " has his fruit unto holiness." – *W. Hubbard.*

And now also the axe is laid - Or, Even now the axe lieth. As if he had said, There is not a moment to spare - God is about to cut off every impenitent soul - you must therefore either turn to God immediately, or be utterly and finally ruined. It was customary with the prophets to represent the kingdoms, nations, and individuals, whose ruin they predicted, under the notion of forests and trees, doomed to be cut down. See

Jer_46:22, Jer_46:23; Eze_31:3, Eze_31:11, Eze_31:12. The Baptist follows the same metaphor: the Jewish nation is the tree, and the Romans the axe, which, by the just judgment of God, was speedily to cut it down. It has been well observed, that there is an allusion here to a woodman, who, having marked a tree for excision, lays his axe at its root, and strips off his outer garment, that he may wield his blows more powerfully, and that his work may be quickly performed. For about sixty years before the coming of Christ, this axe had been lying at the root of the Jewish tree, Judea having been made a province to the Roman empire, from the time that Pompey took the city of Jerusalem, during the contentions of the two brothers Hyrcanus and Aristobulus, which was about sixty-three years before the coming of Christ. See Joseph. Antiq. l. xiv. c. 1-5. But as the country might be still considered as in the hands of the Jews, though subject to the Romans, and God had waited on them now nearly ninety years from the above time, expecting them to bring forth fruit, and none was yet produced; he kept the Romans as an axe, lying at the root of this tree, who were ready to cut it down the moment God gave them the commission. – Adam Clarke

3:11 I indeed baptize you with water unto repentance: but he that cometh after me is mightier than I, whose shoes I am not worthy to bear: he shall baptize you with the Holy Ghost, and *with* fire:

St. Chrysostom says; it means the superabundant graces of the Spirit. Basil and Theophilus explain it of the fire of hell. Cyril, Jerome, and others, understand by it the descent of the Holy Spirit, on the day of

Pentecost.

Origen and Lactantius conceive it to be a river of fire, at the gate of heaven, something similar to the Phlegethon of the heathens; but they observe, that when the righteous come to pass over, the liquid flames shall divide, and give them a free passage: that Christ shall stand on the brink of it, and receive through the flames all those, and none but those, who have received in this world the baptism of water in his name: and that this baptism is for those who, having received the faith of Christ, have not, in every respect, lived conformably to it; for, though they laid the good foundation, yet they built hay, straw, and stubble upon it, and this work of theirs must be tried, and destroyed by this fire. This, they think, is St. Paul's meaning, 1Co_3:13-15. If any man build on this foundation (viz. Jesus Christ) gold, silver, precious stones, wood, hay, stubble; every man's work shall be made manifest: and the fire shall try every man's work, of what sort it is. - If any man's work be burnt, he shall suffer loss: but he himself shall be saved; yet so as By Fire. From this fire, understood in this way, the fathers of the following ages, and the schoolmen, formed the famous and lucrative doctrine of Purgatory. Some in the primitive Church thought that fire should be, in some way or other, joined to the water in baptism; and it is supposed that they administered it by causing the person to pass between two fires, or to leap through the flame; or by having a torch, or lighted candle, present. Thus have those called Doctors of the Church trifled. The exposition which I have given, I believe to be the only genuine one. – Adam Clarke

John did not consider himself to be worthy to be counted

as more than the lowliest of servants; sadly too many of us Christians today are not wise enough to have the humility John did.

The Holy Spirit is fire. Baptism with the Holy Spirit is not one thing and baptism with fire another; the former is the reality of which the latter is the symbol. The Christ plunges us into this fire which transforms and purifies. "The Spirit produces holiness in heart and character. All other cleansing is superficial. The alternative for every man is to be baptized in fire or to be consumed by it." – Dr. MacLaren

3:12 Whose fan *is* in his hand, and he will thoroughly purge his floor, and gather his wheat into the garner; but he will burn up the chaff with unquenchable fire.

Humanity yields its twofold crop, its wheat and its chaff. Sometimes the chaff deceives itself into thinking it is the wheat. Jesus comes to unveil the reality and expose what we are. Whether we want Him or not, He comes "Whose fan is in His hand."

The sifting work must be done not only for the truth's sake, but for the sake of the foolish ones as well as the saved ones and even for the welfare of the world. Otherwise the world goes from bad to worse without respite as it is deluded to destruction.

A calamity comes, the two sorts of men are disclosed. Before hand you could not say for certain which was which because all looked pretty much alike; in the threshing-floor of God the winnowing has begun; the man's character has been exposed.

One person is overtaken by misfortune and is paralyzed

or embittered, and goes down. Another, struck by the same blow, summons something from within, is sweet tempered, hopeful and courageous and, as he descends in style, rises in spiritual stature. The reason prosperity, however measured, seems to enlarge some persons and belittle others is not so much that it actually alters their dimensions as that it exposes what their dimensions are. It is a shaking of His fan.

Now and then a sharp question of right or wrong is thrust in upon a whole community. Everybody must take sides, openly or secretly. The sifting is happening.

Character cannot be completely concealed. The really curious thing about the economy of the creator is that we are all, since Adam, coming into this world as chaff. However each one of us is given the opportunity to accept or reject His transformative power to become the wheat. Everyman, therefore, is as to his moral character what his own behavior and practice makes him.

In the Christian church there is a mixture of nominal and real Christians. For our benefit, we have been forewarned that this would be the case, the Parable of the Tares; Parable of the Wedding Garment; Five Wise and Five Foolish. The false are careless or indifferent, while the true are penitents, believers, new creatures. The head of the Church knows the true character of all. He will separate the precious from the vile. The final end of all will correspond to their character:

1. Examine yourself.
2. Prepare for the judgment.

3:13 Then cometh Jesus from Galilee to Jordan unto

> John, to be baptized of him.
> 3:14 But John forbad him, saying, I have need to be baptized of thee, and comest thou to me?

These words were uttered under the conviction that Jesus was The Christ.

> 3:15 And Jesus answering said unto him, Suffer *it to be so* now: for thus it becometh us to fulfil all righteousness. Then he suffered him.

The implication is that the relation of Jesus to His work made it proper that He should be baptized. Baptism was for sinners; Jesus was sinless but He humbled Himself, and accepted the burden of human duties to set the example.

Jesus obeyed the Jewish Law but not necessarily all of the Pharisaic, although He instructed the Apostles to obey their laws. The reason, in part, was that His knowledge and wisdom is far above ours and therefore He knew which ones could be disregarded, and when, without violating the intent of God's law. Jesus fulfilled every righteous ordinance.

Now as Jesus had submitted to circumcision, which was the initiatory ordinance of the Mosaic dispensation, it was necessary that He should submit to this initiatory ordinance which was instituted by no less an authority, and was the initiatory ordinance of His own dispensation. Additionally Jesus represented the high priest, and was to be the high priest of the house of God. The high priest was initiated into his office by washing and anointing, so must The Christ: He was baptized, washed, and anointed by the Holy Spirit. Thereby He fulfilled the righteous ordinance of His initiation into the office of high priest, and was thus prepared to make atonement for the sins of mankind as none other could.

Unfortunately, some place a far greater emphasis on the water baptism than they should. It has almost no value in the salvation of our soul. Jesus alone saves; it is becoming to us to be baptized as a testimony to others that we are a part of God's forever family, it is a public declaration of devotion to God and therefore necessary, but for those who place their trust in this ordinance for their salvation it becomes essentially worthless, certainly no better than the ritual of hand washing.

> 3:16 And Jesus, when he was baptized, went up straightway out of the water: and, lo, the heavens were opened unto him, and he saw the Spirit of God descending like a dove, and lighting upon him:
> 3:17 And lo a voice from heaven, saying, This is my beloved Son, in whom I am well pleased.

Visible and audible affirmation, although, perhaps, John was the only one who saw the Spirit.

A gentleman, passing a church with Daniel Webster, asked him, "How can you reconcile the doctrine of the Trinity with reason?" The statesman replied by asking, "Do you understand the arithmetic of heaven?" The application is evident. - Anon

CHAPTER FOUR

4:1 Then was Jesus led up of the Spirit into the wilderness to be tempted of the devil.

The first act in the ministry of Jesus The Christ was a combat with Satan. If our Lord had not become incarnate He would never have been tempted, for temptation is not possible to God. God is above the possibility of temptation; the beasts are below it. The possession of an animal nature is not the only source of temptation as some imagine, or the "Angels who kept not their own estate" could never have fallen. The conditions of a moral goodness possible to a creature involve the possibility of its opposite.

The evangelists were thoroughly convinced of the reality of the temptation; lesser men have tried to dismiss it. His temptations came from without, not from within Him. An inward bias towards evil is not essential to temptation; temptation may appeal to what is best within us, to satisfy lawful appetites by unlawful means.

> The tempter's power is limited by the fact that he is a mere creature and by the providence of God. We ought not to exaggerate the power of Satan, let us beware of underrating it. – Norman MacLeod, D.D.

> 4:2 And when he had fasted forty days and forty nights, he was afterward an hungred.
> 4:3 And when the tempter came to him, he said, If thou be the Son of God, command that these stones be made bread.
> 4:4 But he answered and said, It is written, Man shall not live by bread alone, but by every word that proceedeth out of the mouth of God.

Jesus is urged to satisfy His hunger by working a miracle. He refused because miraculous power must not be used simply for personal advantage.

> 4:5 Then the devil taketh him up into the holy city, and setteth him on a pinnacle of the temple,
> 4:6 And saith unto him, If thou be the Son of God, cast thyself down: for it is written, He shall give his angels charge concerning thee: and in *their* hands they shall bear thee up, lest at any time thou dash thy foot against a stone.

Scripture may be misapplied to lead us into sin. The devil and many of his emissaries are expert in that endeavor. Resistance to temptation is aided by an accurate familiarity with God's word.

> 4:7 Jesus said unto him, It is written again, Thou shalt not tempt the Lord thy God.
> 4:8 Again, the devil taketh him up into an exceeding high mountain, and sheweth him all the kingdoms of the

world, and the glory of them;
4:9 And saith unto him, All these things will I give thee, if thou wilt fall down and worship me.
4:10 Then saith Jesus unto him, Get thee hence, Satan: for it is written, Thou shalt worship the Lord thy God, and him only shalt thou serve.
4:11 Then the devil leaveth him, and, behold, angels came and ministered unto him.

The threefold temptation by Satan results in a threefold victory over Satan. Whenever I resist a temptation from Satan I gain a victory over him also. Of course I probably only rate a minor demon but it is a victory over the unholy kingdom, nevertheless and cause for a celebration for I know Whom has empowered me for the victory.

Jesus' victory was won in spite of the repeated onsets of the devil who had tried every avenue of approach. The issues at stake were of vast import as the champions of light and darkness grappled for the mastery of men. Luke 4:13 adds that the devil left Jesus only "Until a more opportune time."

4:12 Now when Jesus had heard that John was cast into prison, he departed into Galilee;

A bit of time passes between this and the previous verse. If not for the fourth gospel we might not be aware that several months passed between the baptism of Jesus and the imprisonment of John. At the time of Jesus' baptism John is still too popular for Herod to have hazarded his arrest and imprisonment. As the months pass John's popularity wanes but the people in Jerusalem are failing to respond to their Messiah and they squander the special opportunity presented to them so He goes to the part of the land the elitists consider barely part of the Land at all.

Though John is in prison and seemingly failure has been written on the work of his life that is only superficial.. While the multitudes that had been stirred by his ministry have relapsed back to their old indifference there are some souls who have been permanently touched by his preaching.

> 4:13 And leaving Nazareth, he came and dwelt in Capernaum, which is upon the sea coast, in the borders of Zabulon and Nephthalim:
> 4:14 That it might be fulfilled which was spoken by Esaias the prophet, saying,
> 4:15 The land of Zabulon, and the land of Nephthalim, *by* the way of the sea, beyond Jordan, Galilee of the Gentiles;
> 4:16 The people which sat in darkness saw great light; and to them which sat in the region and shadow of death light is sprung up.
> 4:17 From that time Jesus began to preach, and to say, Repent: for the kingdom of heaven is at hand.
> 4:18 And Jesus, walking by the sea of Galilee, saw two brethren, Simon called Peter, and Andrew his brother, casting a net into the sea: for they were fishers.

The Galilean fishermen's hearts had been prepared by the preaching of the prophet John who was preparing the path for the Lamb of God, the King of Kings, The Messiah, the Great Shepherd. They were ready. The Holy One of Nazareth is walking by the shores of their lake. Nothing in His appearance betrays who He is but their ears perk up at The Shepherd's voice.

Seminaries of learning , in the order of God's providence and grace, have great and important use and should be treated with great respect. Man's seminary in Jerusalem had become quite corrupted and Jesus brings these men into His uncorrupted personally run seminary to properly prepare them to preach His good news.

4:19 And he saith unto them, Follow me, and I will make you fishers of men.

Follow Me – Receive my doctrines, imitate Me in My conduct and in every way be My disciples.

and I will make you fishers of men — raising them from a lower to a higher *fishing,* as David was from a lower to a higher *feeding* (Psa_78:70-72). – Jamieson, Fausset and Brown Commentary

4:20 And they straightway left *their* nets, and followed him.
4:21 And going on from thence, he saw other two brethren, James *the son* of Zebedee, and John his brother, in a ship with Zebedee their father, mending their nets; and he called them.
4:22 And they immediately left the ship and their father, and followed him.
4:23 And Jesus went about all Galilee, teaching in their synagogues, and preaching the gospel of the kingdom, and healing all manner of sickness and all manner of disease among the people.

Healing for all – I remember, when the Master Street Hospital, in Philadelphia, was opened during the war, a telegram came saying, "There will be three hundred wounded men tonight; be ready to take care of them;" and from my church there went in some twenty or thirty men and women to look after these poor wounded fellows. As they came, some from one part of the land, some from another, no one asked whether this man was from Oregon, or from Massachusetts, or from Minnesota, or from New York. There was a wounded soldier, and the only question was how to take off the rags the most gently, and put on the bandage, and administer the cordial. And when a soul comes to God, he does not ask where you came from, or what your ancestry was. Healing for all your wounds. Pardon for all your guilt. Comfort for all your troubles. – *Dr. Talmage.*

4:24 And his fame went throughout all Syria: and they brought unto him all sick people that were taken with divers diseases and torments, and those which were possessed with devils, and those which were lunatick, and those that had the palsy; and he healed them.

Torments – colics, gouts, and rheumatisms

Devils – demoniacs. Persons possessed by evil spirits. This is the plain and obvious meaning of the word "demoniac" in the Gospels. Many think that the sacred writers simply followed the unfounded prejudices of the common people by attributing certain diseases to the influence of evil spirits which were actually the effects of natural causes: but their "enlightened" viewpoint is based upon their failure to pay careful attention to details provided in the accounts as well as the rest of God's word. While there are multitudes of demons or evil spirits, there is, properly speaking, only one Devil who seems to be the head over all the rest. He is the chief accuser or slanderer. He accused, slandered, God in paradise as being opposed to the increase of man's knowledge and happiness, even as his agents do to this day. Additionally, he is the accuser of men

Revelation 12:9-10 and Job 1:7.

4:25 And there followed him great multitudes of people from Galilee, and *from* Decapolis, and *from* Jerusalem, and *from* Judaea, and *from* beyond Jordan.

CHAPTER FIVE

5:1 And seeing the multitudes, he went up into a mountain: and when he was set, his disciples came unto him:

The multitudes mentioned in 4:25. It is not one of the "Holy" mountains; it is actually quite probable that nothing more is meant than a fair sized hill. He seated himself, following the pattern of the rabbis, as He began to teach that day. Some have suggested this "mountain" or that other mountain without any legitimacy for their argument because it is His teaching, not the location, which is of importance.

The hearers were primarily His disciples who followed Him for love and learning while the masses followed only for the cures. His disciples would understand and obey, while the others would consider this sermon extraneous to their concerns and of little value. Some of those in the multitude may have "remembered" some shopping they needed to get done because, after all, they had already been to Sabbath Services recently.

5:2 And he opened his mouth, and taught them, saying,

> 5:3 Blessed *are* the poor in spirit: for theirs is the kingdom of heaven.

Not to be confused with poor in worldly circumstances but the one who is aware of his own spiritual poverty and seeking out the means to remedy his inadequate standing with God. All without Christ Jesus are wretched, blind, naked, poor. The prevenient grace of God awakens us to our condition and the means of His grace.

> 5:4 Blessed *are* they that mourn: for they shall be comforted.

This verse is frequently misapplied at funerals as it is for those who feel their spiritual poverty and lament the iniquity that separates from the fountain of blessedness. Not the sorrow in adversity, not the sorrow because of disappointed hopes, not the sorrow over temporal distress. It is only such persons as are deeply convinced of the sinfulness of sin, who feel the plague of their own heart, and turn with disgust from all worldly consolations, because of their insufficiency to render them happy; they are the ones who have God's solid promise of comfort spoken of here.

They shall have the clearer views of Christ Jesus and His grace and presence.

> 5:5 Blessed *are* the meek: for they shall inherit the earth.

In opposition to the proud and supercilious Scribes and Pharisees and their disciples.

> 5:6 Blessed *are* they which do hunger and thirst after righteousness: for they shall be filled.

When a soul is awakened to a sense of its needs and to

seek and hunger and thirst after righteousness or holiness, which is its proper food we know that it will be purified by the Holy Spirit and be filled by the living bread to completeness.

The first four beatitudes present the pre-saints as conscious of their need of salvation and the acting suitably to that character rather than in the possession of it. The next three beatitudes present the saint as having now found salvation and conducting themselves accordingly.

> 5:7 Blessed *are* the merciful: for they shall obtain mercy.

Christ did not mean for a man to be merciful merely for the sake of obtaining mercy but mercy is a reward of mercy. It is reflected in sorrow at the suffering of a fellow creature accompanied with a desire to alleviate the suffering and even the potential suffering which may result due to the fellow creature's wrong choices. This grace is obligatory because of the mercy we have received.

> Mercy is not purchased but at the price of mercy itself; and even this price is a gift of the mercy of God. What mercy can those vindictive persons expect, who forgive nothing, and are always ready to improve every advantage they have of avenging themselves? Whatever mercy a man shows to another, God will take care to show the same to him. – Adam Clarke

> 5:8 Blessed *are* the pure in heart: for they shall see God.

Now this is by no means restricted to moral purity, it denotes one who has allowed himself to be completely consecrated to Christ so that his inward nature corresponds with his outward profession. Isaiah 29:13; Psalm 24: 3-5.

What begins as an instantaneous act of the Spirit of God must be maintained in the day by day walk with the Holy Spirit as an essential to growth in the graces of saintliness as physical food is to the physical body. Purity is maintained only by abiding in The Christ.

Shall see God – A Hebraism meaning possessing it, abiding with. John 3:3 "Except a man be born again, he cannot see the kingdom of God," i.e. cannot enter heaven/possess it as his eternal home. Further strengthened by John 3:18, "He that believeth on him [Jesus] is not condemned: but he that believeth not is condemned already, because he hath not believed in the name of the only begotten Son of God."

In contrast to the Pharisee who manifested outward purity while his heart was full of corruption and defilement, Christ claims that a purification of the heart is an essentiality in order to enter into the kingdom of God.

> 5:9 Blessed *are* the peacemakers: for they shall be called the children of God.

Peacemakers – real peacemakers strive to bring others to a knowledge of Jesus who is the source of true peace.

The world is full of peace-breakers; some of them even claim to be Christian; let God be their judge and may He bring swift justice upon them so that, perhaps, they may repent. The peace a godly person seeks does not permit compromise with sinners although we are to be peaceable with their person. Although it sounds overly simplistic, "Hate the sin, not the sinner." Pray for, counsel, relieve them, but take care not to catch their infection.

We have to be careful to avoid becoming so enamored of

the golden crown of peace that we cast aside the far more costly treasure of truth. Better to let peace go than truth.

Before people can become true peacemakers and be entitled to the promise in this beatitude they must seek and obtain inward peace for themselves. Following that then it becomes their duty to promote peace and restore it where it is lacking whether it is between man and God or between man and man. See Romans 12:18.

True children of God obey God out of love. If you don't have time for Church then you have the problem and it is not the church that has the problem.

> 5:10 Blessed *are* they which are persecuted for righteousness' sake: for theirs is the kingdom of heaven.

That is because they have, or pursue, the righteousness described by Jesus the Messiah. Posing as persecuted is a favorite stunt among so many. However the kingdom of Heaven belongs only to those who suffer for the sake of goodness, not they who are guilty of wrong or are in the habit of blaming others for their failures when they themselves have failed to make use of whatever means to better their own self. The one who is truly a righteous person, the one who mourns because of any remaining unrighteousness found within himself and is pure in heart, yes, all they that would live godly in and for Jesus shall suffer persecution in this world, according to Jesus. Folks, 2nd Timothy 3:12 hasn't been erased from the Bible in spite of the claims of the "Prosperity Gospel" preachers who attempt to teach such things as, "Job caused his own problems by negative thoughts and could have avoided all that calamity which befell him by keeping a positive mental attitude." The world will always say, away with such fellows who won't follow our different interpretation and "March to our drum." Their lives are not like those who are more easily manipulated and they reprove our thoughts and they are odious to us.

They which are persecuted - Δεδιωγμενοι, they who are hard pressed upon and pursued with repeated acts of enmity. Parkhurst. They are happy who suffer, seems a strange saying: and that the righteous should suffer, merely because they are such, seems as strange. But such is the enmity of the human heart to every thing of God and goodness, that all those who live godly in Christ Jesus shall suffer persecution in one form or other. As the religion of Christ gives no quarter to vice, so the vicious will give no quarter to this religion, or to its professors. – Adam Clarke

5:11 Blessed are ye, when *men* shall revile you, and persecute *you,* and shall say all manner of evil against you falsely, for my sake.

When men shall revile you, and persecute - The persecution mentioned in the preceding verse comprehends all outward acts of violence - all that the hand can do. This comprehends all calumny, slander, etc., all that the tongue can effect. But as διωκειν, which we render to persecute, is a forensic term, and signifies legal persecutions and public accusations, which, though totally unsubstantiated, were the means of destroying multitudes of the primitive Christians, our Lord probably refers to such. No Protestant can think, without horror, of the great numbers burnt alive in this country, on such accusations, under the popish reign of her who is emphatically called Bloody Queen Mary. –

Adam Clarke

The folly and wickedness of those who inflict persecution: It is contrary to sound reason, contrary to sound policy, contrary to Scripture, and it is virtually aimed at The Christ. Generally speaking, the perpetrator/s doesn't/don't know, although some do, sort of, that they are opposing the creator of the universe.

> 5:12 Rejoice, and be exceeding glad: for great *is* your reward in heaven: for so persecuted they the prophets which were before you.

2nd Chronicles 36:16 But they mocked God's messengers, despised his words and scoffed at his prophets until the wrath of the Lord was aroused against his people and there was no remedy.

The reward of the saints: It is even over and above the happiness that naturally and directly flows from holiness. Remember who bestows it. We may see some of it in this life as a down payment, but its greatest fulfillment is eternal.

God gives the grace to endure suffering and then crowns that grace with glory; therefore the reward is not of debt, but of grace.

> 5:13 Ye are the salt of the earth: but if the salt have lost his savor, wherewith shall it be salted? it is thenceforth good for nothing, but to be cast out, and to be trodden under foot of men.

All true believers in Jesus The Christ are delineated as the "salt of the earth" because that which is Divine and holy and precious exists in them and in them only. "Ye" - not the Apostles only, not ministers only; but all followers of Jesus who are pursuing holiness of heart and life are the salt of the earth to season others.

Here we have Jesus' sublime definition of the Christian life. The church exists more for the world's sake more so than for its own. The Christ's followers are to be the "saviors" of others. We Christians are not called for our own comfort, but to show others the beauty of the divine life and to raise them to the same or higher level.

Salt is intended to nourish: it is an article of food.

Salt is intended to preserve, to delay corruption.

Salt has antiseptic qualities, when laid on a wound it is painful. Sometimes the Christian causes pain in the process of promoting healing.

Followers of Jesus should seek to prevent the corruption of literature, to prevent the corruption of public amusements, to prevent the corruption of private and public life, to prevent the corruption of commercial life.

The founders of the USA said that only good and godly men and women should be permitted to hold political offices; interestingly enough, all the bad things in American history can be traced back to failure to keep the corrupt ones out of those positions of influence.

It is the power and obligation of the good to arrest corruption by their own purity. The Christian, by his example ought to bring out the best in the people with whom he comes into contact.

But if the salt have lost his savor - Mr. Maundrell, who, describing the Valley of Salt, speaks thus: "Along, on one side of the valley, toward Gibul, there is a small precipice about two men's lengths, occasioned by the continual taking away of the salt; and, in this, you may see how the veins of it lie. I broke a piece of it, of which that part that was exposed to the rain, sun, and air, though it had the sparks and particles of salt, Yet It Had Perfectly Lost Its Savor: the inner part, which was connected to the rock, retained its savor, as I found by proof." See his Trav., 5th edit., last page. A preacher, or private Christian, who has lost the life of Christ, and the witness of his Spirit, out of his soul, may be likened to this salt. He may have the sparks and glittering particles of true wisdom, but without its unction or comfort. Only that which is connected with the rock, the soul that is in union with Christ Jesus by the Holy Spirit, can preserve its savor, and be instrumental of good to others. - Adam Clarke Commentary

Every person, apart from Christ, is the salt that is without savor, no matter how good that person may seem to other people; but God, against all logic, is willing to impart to them, if they be willing to accept, that which will give them the character and properties needed to make them "Salt of the earth;" just as he did for us who have become followers of The Christ.

To be trodden underfoot - There was a species of salt in Judea, which was generated at the lake Asphaltites, and hence called bituminous salt, easily rendered vapid, and of no other use but to be spread in a part of the temple, to prevent slipping in wet weather. This is probably what our Lord alludes to in this place. The existence of such a salt, and its application to such a use, Schoettgenius has largely proved in his Horae Hebraicae, vol. i. p. 18, etc. –Adam Clarke Commentary

Hebrews 10:29 Of how much sorer punishment, suppose ye, shall he be thought worthy, who hath trodden underfoot the Son of God, and hath counted the blood of the covenant, wherewith he was sanctified, an unholy thing, and hath done despite unto the Spirit of grace?

> 5:14 Ye are the light of the world. A city that is set on an hill cannot be hid.

The world is dark – morally dark.

Light of the world – was a title applied to the most eminent Rabbins. Christ transfers the title from them and gives it to His own disciples, who, by doctrines He taught, were to be the means of sending the light of life throughout the world. Kindled by the Son we are to cast light upon the whole world.

> Quesnell remarks here: "The Christian life is something very high and sublime, to which we cannot arrive without pains: while it withdraws us from the earth, and carries us nearer heaven, it places us in view, and as a mark, to the malice of carnal men." – Adam Clarke Commentary

By being the salt and light Jesus has called His followers to be, we incur the hatred of some men but there are others whose feeble light is strengthened and thus are they emboldened to burn brighter to the glory of God.

> 5:15 Neither do men light a candle, and put it under a bushel, but on a candlestick; and it giveth light unto all that are in the house.

> From some ancient writers we learn, that only those who had bad designs hid a candle under a bushel; that,

in the dead of the night, when all were asleep, they might rise up, and have light at hand to help them to effect their horrid purposes of murder, etc. See Wetstein, Kypke, Wolf, etc. – Adam Clarke Commentary

5:16 Let your light so shine before men, that they may see your good works, and glorify your Father which is in heaven.

Let every follower of Christ, and especially every preacher of the Gospel, disperse the light of heavenly knowledge, and the warmth of Divine love through the whole circle of their acquaintance. Our whole conduct should be a perpetual comment on the grace and doctrine we have received, and be a constant exemplification of its power and truth. Real Christians are the children of God - they are partakers of his holy and happy nature: they should ever be concerned for their Father's honor, and endeavor so to recommend him, and his salvation, that others may be prevailed on to come to the light, and walk in it.

Claimants of Christianity, who live like other men give evidence that they have not been renewed in spirit. It is a strange thing how some of them will self-justify by claiming to be under grace, not the law so that they can continue on with their favorite sins because they have uttered the "Magic phrase," "I believe in Jesus," therefore all of my sins, past, present and future are as if they never happened.

Consistency in the Christian walk is very needful; the cause of Christ is greatly harmed when we fail to be Christ-like and then try to dismiss that failure with such phrases as, "I'm only a sinner saved by grace." The problem lies herein; to the person who is not a Christ follower that sounds very much like "There is nothing special about Christ Jesus," which means you are bearing God's name in vain. Christian consistency glorifies our Heavenly Father and breaks down many barriers to His influence others have erected and improves the chances that they may be led to embrace Jesus for themselves as Savior also.

5:17 Think not that I am come to destroy the law, or the prophets: I am not come to destroy, but to fulfill.

These words teach us the permanent authority of the moral principles of the Jewish Law. He was like a painter laying fresh colors upon an old picture.

5:18 For verily I say unto you, Till heaven and earth pass, one jot or one tittle shall in no wise pass from the law, till all be fulfilled.

That this saying, one jot or one tittle, is a proverbial mode of expression among the Jews, and that it expressed the meaning given to it above, is amply proved by the extracts in Lightfoot and Schoettgen. The reader will not be displeased to find a few of them here, if he can bear with the allegorical and strongly figurative language of the rabbins.

In Shir Hashirim Rabba, are these words:

> "Should all the inhabitants of the earth gather together, in order to whiten one feather of a crow, they could not succeed: so, if all the inhabitants of the earth should unite to abolish one ׳ yod, which is the smallest letter in the whole law, they should not be able to effect it."

In Vayikra Rabba, s. 19, it is said:

"Should any person in the words of Deu_6:4, Hear, O Israel, the Lord our God is אחד achad, One Lord, change the ד daleth into a ר resh, he would ruin the world." [Because, in that case, the word אחר achar, would signify a strange or false God].

"Should any one, in the words of Exo_34:14, Thou shalt worship no Other, אחר achar, God, change ר resh into ד daleth, he would ruin the world." [Because the command would then run, Thou shalt not worship the Only or true God].

"Should any one in the words of Lev_22:32, Neither shall ye Profane תחללו techelelu, my holy name, change ח cheth into ה he, he would ruin the world." [Because the sense of the commandment would then be, Neither shall ye Praise my holy name].

"Should any one, in the words of Psa_150:6, Let every thing that hath breath Praise, תהלל tehalel, the Lord, change ה, he into ח cheth, he would ruin the world." [Because the command would then run, Let every thing that hath breath Profane the Lord].

"Should any one, in the words of Jer_5:10, They lied Against the Lord, ביהוה beihovah, change ב beth into כ caph, he would ruin the world." [For then the words would run, They lied Like the Lord].

"Should any one, in the words of Hosea, Hos_5:7, They have dealt treacherously, ביהוה beihovah, Against the Lord, change ב beth into כ caph, he would ruin the world." [For then the words would run, They have dealt treacherously Like the Lord].

"Should any one, in the words of 1Sa_2:2, There is

none holy As the Lord, change כ caph into ב beth, he would ruin the world." [For then the words would mean, There is no holiness In the Lord].

These examples fully prove that the μια κεραια of our Lord, refers to the apices, points, or corners, that distinguish ב beth from כ caph; ח cheth from ה he; and ר resh from ד daleth. For the reader will at once perceive, how easily a כ caph may be turned into a ב beth; a ה he into a ח cheth; and a ר resh into a ד daleth: and he will also see of what infinite consequence it is to write and print such letters correctly.

Till all be fulfilled - Or, accomplished. Though all earth and hell should join together to hinder the accomplishment of the great designs of the Most High, yet it shall all be in vain - even the sense of a single letter shall not be lost. The words of God, which point out his designs, are as unchangeable as his nature itself. Every sinner, who perseveres in his iniquity, shall surely be punished with separation from God and the glory of his power; and every soul that turns to God, through Christ, shall as surely be saved, as that Jesus himself hath died. – Adam Clarke Commentary

5:19 Whosoever therefore shall break one of these least commandments, and shall teach men so, he shall be called the least in the kingdom of heaven: but whosoever shall do and teach *them,* the same shall be called great in the kingdom of heaven.

Jesus puts practice above profession. The Scribes and Pharisees were men who "say and do not" (Matthew 23:3)

The Pharisees were notorious for making a distinction between weightier and lighter matters in the law, and between what has been called, in a certain part of the Christian Church, mortal and venial sins. See more at Matthew 22:36.

Whosoever shall break – He who, by his mode of acting, speaking, or explaining the words of God, sets the holy precept aside, or explains away its force and meaning, shall be called least – shall be excluded from the kingdom of heaven.

Little sins leave men barely aware that they have broken God's law; great sins stir up piercing thoughts. The great peril of little sins is they are sure to draw greater ones after them as the conscious becomes desensitized. Christ does not authorize us to suppose that any of His commands be little.

> 5:20 For I say unto you, That except your righteousness shall exceed *the righteousness* of the scribes and Pharisees, ye shall in no case enter into the kingdom of heaven.

Our minimum must exceed their maximum. Christianity must be practiced from the inside out; the Pharisees practiced their religion from the outside and didn't worry too much about the inside – sort of an "I sin daily in thought and word, but my deeds look okay" ideology.

Jesus calls for a righteousness that exceeds that of the most scrupulous moralist. All other righteousness does the orders of God: this does His will. It is a righteousness that is possessed as well as imputed. The Pharisee's and the Christian's conduct appear the same but the Christian's righteousness comes from the heart. Not mere outward zeal for the law, but inward conformity. Theirs was a servile righteousness ours is to be originating in love.

> A shipmaster wants to anchor. He throws out his anchor, and puts out his cable, and comes within about twenty feet of the bottom. It is not any longer. What is it good for? It is good as far as it goes; but it does not go far enough to touch the bottom, and therefore it is not good for anything. – H. W. Beecher.

5:21 Ye have heard that it was said by them of old time, Thou shalt not kill; and whosoever shall kill shall be in danger of the judgment:

Ye have heard that it was said by them of old time - τοις αρχαιοις, to or by the ancients. By the ancients, we may understand those who lived before the law, and those who lived under it; for murder was, in the most solemn manner, forbidden before, as well as under, the law, Gen_9:5, Gen_9:6.

But it is very likely that our Lord refers here merely to traditions and glosses relative to the ancient Mosaic ordinance; and such as, by their operation, rendered the primitive command of little or no effect. Murder from the beginning has been punished with death; and it is, probably, the only crime that should be punished with death. There is much reason to doubt, whether the punishment of death, inflicted for any other crime, is not in itself murder, whatever the authority may be that has instituted it. God, and the greatest legislators that have ever been in the universe, are of the same opinion. See Montesquieu, Blackstone, and the Marquis Beccaria, and the arguments and testimonies lately produced by

Sir Samuel Romilly, in his motion for the amendment of the criminal laws of this kingdom. It is very remarkable, that the criminal code published by Joseph II., late emperor of Germany, though it consists of seventy-one capital crimes, has not death attached to any of them. Even murder, with all intention to rob, is punished only with "imprisonment for thirty years, to lie on the floor, to have no nourishment but bread and water, to be closely chained, and to be publicly whipped once a year, with less than one hundred lashes." See Colquhoun on the Police of the City of London, p. 272. – Adam Clarke Commentary

5:22 But I say unto you, That whosoever is angry with his brother without a cause shall be in danger of the judgment: and whosoever shall say to his brother, Raca, shall be in danger of the council: but whosoever shall say, Thou fool, shall be in danger of hell fire.

Restraint of hasty temper possible

La Fontaine, chaplain of the Prussian army, once preached an earnest sermon on the sin and folly of yielding to a hasty temper. The next day a Major of the regiment accosted him in no very good humour, saying: "Well, sir! I think you made use of the prerogative of your office to annoy me with some very sharp hits yesterday." "I certainly thought of you while I was preparing the sermon," the chaplain answered, "but I had no intention of being personal or sharp." "Well, it is of no use," said the Major, "I have a hasty temper, and I cannot help it. I cannot control it; the thing is impossible." The following Sunday La Fontaine preached on self-deception, and the vain excuses which men are accustomed to make. "Why." said he, "a man will declare it is impossible to control his temper, when he very well knows that were the same provocation to happen in the presence of his sovereign, he not only *could,* but *would* control himself entirely. And yet he dares to say that the continual presence of the King of kings imposes upon him neither restraint nor fear." The next day the preacher met the officer again, who said, humbly, "You were right yesterday, chaplain. Hereafter, whenever you see me in the danger of falling, remind me of The King."

5:23 Therefore if thou bring thy gift to the altar, and there rememberest that thy brother hath ought against thee;
5:24 Leave there thy gift before the altar, and go thy way; first be reconciled to thy brother, and then come and offer thy gift.

Evil must be nipped in the bud. An unkind thought of another may be the foundation of that which leads to actual murder. A Christian, properly speaking, cannot be an enemy to any man; nor is he to consider any man his enemy, without the fullest evidence: for surmises to the prejudice of another can never rest in the bosom of him who has the love of God in his heart, for to him all men are brethren. He sees all men as children of God, and members of Christ, or at least capable of becoming such. If a tender forgiving spirit was required, even in a Jew, when he approached God's altar with a bullock or a lamb, how much more necessary is this in a man who professes to be a follower of the Lamb of

God; especially when he receives the symbols of that Sacrifice which was offered for the life of the world, in what is commonly called the sacrament of the Lord's supper! – Adam Clarke Commentary

> 5:25 Agree with thine adversary quickly, whiles thou art in the way with him; lest at any time the adversary deliver thee to the judge, and the judge deliver thee to the officer, and thou be cast into prison.

> A good use of this very prudential advice of our Lord is this: Thou art a sinner; God hath a controversy with thee. There is but a step between thee and death. Now is the accepted time. Thou art invited to return to God by Christ Jesus. Come immediately at his call, and he will save thy soul. Delay not! Eternity is at hand; and if thou die in thy sins, where God is thou shalt never come. – Adam Clarke Commentary

> 5:26 Verily I say unto thee, Thou shalt by no means come out thence, till thou hast paid the uttermost farthing.

> 5:27 Ye have heard that it was said by them of old time, Thou shalt not commit adultery:
> 5:28 But I say unto you, That whosoever looketh on a woman to lust after her hath committed adultery with her already in his heart.

Like murder, adultery is the final fruit of wrong thoughts and uncontrolled feelings.

> The depraved heart is before God of the same criminality as the depraved life, and exposes us to the same punishment from God. Let us therefore eternally renounce every inclination inconsistent with [the

Christian] religion and reproachful to humanity. Let us cultivate purity of heart. – *David Lamont, D.D.*

Actions are the public representations of our private sentiments. Those still of a corrupt nature tend to quickly object to the prohibition of heart adultery. However, the one who wrote the Seventh Commandment is the one who was explaining its meaning and intention that day on the mount.

There are those who cheer when they see or hear of a person of God stumble because they have an animosity towards anyone who proclaims the reality of God's high moral expectations of anyone who hopes to enter heaven as if God grades on a curve and they might have a chance to get by with their favorite sin if only everyone else would participate in their sin.

Victory over the desires of the heart must be accomplished even if it means stress and pain. Everything given by the grace of God is to save us from our sins, not in them; there is no record of Jesus ever telling anyone, "Try not to sin as much as you used to," it was always "Sin no more," i.e. "stop sinning." Those who lead others into temptation to sin by whatever method make themselves guilty accomplices of the sin, and will be held accountable.

If one is willing to submit to the operating knives of human doctors in order to save their life should they not submit more readily to the Divine Being's requirements? After all He will give grace and consolations via His Spirit.

> 5:29 And if thy right eye offend thee, pluck it out, and cast *it* from thee: for it is profitable for thee that one of thy members should perish, and not *that* thy whole body should be cast into hell.

Jesus was not teaching self-mutilation as some mistakenly interpret this.

> 5:30 And if thy right hand offend thee, cut it off, and cast *it* from thee: for it is profitable for thee that one of thy members should perish, and not *that* thy whole body should be cast into hell.

> **pluck it out and cast it from thee** — implying a certain indignant promptitude, heedless of whatever cost to feeling the act may involve. Of course, it is not *the eye simply* of which our Lord speaks - as if execution were to be done upon the bodily organ - though there have been fanatical ascetics who have both advocated and practiced this, showing a very low apprehension of spiritual things - but *the offending eye,* or the eye considered as the occasion of sin; and consequently, only the *sinful exercise* of the organ which is meant. For as one might put out his eyes without in the least quenching the lust to which they ministered, so, "if thine eye be single, thy whole body shall be full of light," and, when directed by a holy mind, becomes an "instrument of righteousness unto God." At the same time, just as by cutting off a hand, or plucking out an eye, the *power* of acting and of seeing would be destroyed, our Lord certainly means that we are to *strike at the root* of such unholy dispositions, as well as cut off the occasions which tend to stimulate them. – Jamiesson, Fausset, Brown Commentary

Men often part with some members of the body, at the discretion of a surgeon, that they may preserve the trunk, and die a little later; and yet they will not deprive themselves of a look, a touch, a small pleasure, which endanger the eternal death of the soul. It is not enough to shut the eye, or stop the hand; the one must be plucked out, and the other cut off. Neither is this enough, we must cast them both from us. Not one moment's truce with an evil passion, or a sinful appetite. If you indulge them, they will gain strength, and you shall be ruined. The rabbins have a saying similar to this: "It is better for thee to be scorched with a little fire in this world, than to be burned with a devouring fire in the world to come." – Adam Clarke Commentary

5:31 It hath been said, Whosoever shall put away his wife, let him give her a writing of divorcement:

Whosoever shall put away his wife - The Jewish doctors gave great license in the matter of divorce. Among them, a man might divorce his wife if she displeased him even in the dressing of his victuals!

Rabbi Akiba said, "If any man saw a woman handsomer than his own wife, he might put his wife away; because it is said in the law, If she find not favor in his eyes." Deu_24:1.

Josephus, the celebrated Jewish historian, in his Life, tells us, with the utmost coolness and indifference, "About this time I put away my wife, who had borne me three children, not being pleased with her manners."

These two cases are sufficient to show to what a scandalous and criminal excess this matter was carried among the Jews. However, it was allowed by the school of Shammai, that no man was to put away his wife unless for adultery. The school of Hillel gave much greater license. – Adam Clarke Commentary

5:32 But I say unto you, That whosoever shall put

away his wife, saving for the cause of fornication,
causeth her to commit adultery: and whosoever shall
marry her that is divorced committeth adultery.

The one legitimate ground for divorce allowed by Deuteronomy 24:1, the "uncleanness," was adultery. One school of interpreters, that of Shammai, explained this correctly but another school, that of Hillel, stretched the expression to the most absurd and frivolous of meanings. Of course, sinful men are prone to go with the latter but Jesus pointed out, without naming names, that God's intent was more accurately reflected by the former. Moses had introduced the law of divorce to prevent easy divorce and protect innocent partners. Corrupted teachers twisted the law to allow easy divorce and therefore Jesus referred them back to God's original standard.

> 5:33 Again, ye have heard that it hath been said by
> them of old time, Thou shalt not forswear thyself, but
> shalt perform unto the Lord thine oaths:

The Society of Friends and a few other ultra-moralists mistakenly think that this statement by Jesus is meant to condemn swearing, oath taking, of every kind and on every occasion but such is, quite logically, not the case. Remember, God Himself is said to have sworn by Himself on more than one occasion. Jesus answered upon oath a question put to Him by the high priest.

Perjury, false oaths, was the prime prohibition in the Old Testament passages but our Lord extends forbidden oaths to all frivolous oaths. In that day, when the Sermon on the Mount was delivered, frivolous oaths were condemned but there were so many caveats that hardly anything, short of having God's name in it, came under that classification.

Jesus expects His followers to be known as truth tellers. Taqqiya or deceit, however you wish to call lying, is not acceptable in those who desire to spend eternity with the Messiah who is the holy one of God and our example.

5:34 But I say unto you, Swear not at all; neither by heaven; for it is God's throne:

Neither by heaven, etc. - It was a custom among the Scythians, when they wished to bind themselves in the most solemn manner, to swear by the king's throne; and if the king was at any time sick, they believed it was occasioned by some one's having taken the oath falsely. Herod. I. iv.

Who is there among the traders and people of this world who obey this law? A common swearer is constantly perjuring himself: such a person should never be trusted. When we make any promise contrary to the command of God, taking, as a pledge of our sincerity, either God, or something belonging to him, we engage that which is not ours, without the Master's consent. God manifests his glory in heaven, as upon his throne; he imprints the footsteps of his perfections upon the earth, his footstool; and shows that his holiness and his grace reign in his temple as the place of his residence. Let it be our constant care to seek and honor God in all his works. – Adam Clarke

5:35 Nor by the earth; for it is his footstool: neither by Jerusalem; for it is the city of the great King.
5:36 Neither shalt thou swear by thy head, because thou canst not make one hair white or black.
5:37 But let your communication be, Yea, yea; Nay, nay: for whatsoever is more than these cometh of evil.

The sin of committing perjury is said to be growing appallingly more frequent. If lies were not so common, oaths would be needless. Muslims can lie with impunity because their religion is based on deception. Followers of the Holy One of God, Messiah Jesus, are to be truthful because their faith is in the one who does not deceive: Titus 1:2; Hebrews 6:18

Allah is best deceiver – Surah 3:54; 8:30; 10:21 and many other passages in the Koran. Therefore, when Muslims lie they are being just like the one they believe in. When Christians lie they are doing dishonor to the one they claim they believe in.

The one true God, who is holy and just, will hold perjurers and those who practice taqqiya accountable before His bar. "And all liars shall have their part in the lake which burns with fire...." – Revelation 21:8

> 5:38 Ye have heard that it hath been said, An eye for an eye, and a tooth for a tooth:
> 5:39 But I say unto you, That ye resist not evil: but whosoever shall smite thee on thy right cheek, turn to him the other also.

The law regarding retaliation was a restriction upon unrestrained vengeance so that the punishment fit the crime and therefore a more humane way of behavior than men were prone to engage in if left to their own devices. The quotation was from Exodus 21:24 and it was intended as a rule for civilized justice. The punishment was not to exceed the crime and personal retaliation was not condoned by it. This *Lex talionis*, the law of like for like, later prevailed among the Greeks and Romans and it prevails, more or less, in most civilized countries even now. The magistrate awarded the punishment when the fact was proved.

Enemies of the Holy Bible have been known to misrepresent the purpose of this law and denigrate it which becomes especially curious when those same individuals then turn around and attempt to embrace the precepts of Islam and Sharia in the name of "tolerance" and "inclusiveness". George Orwell stated, "The further a society drifts from truth, the more it will hate those that speak it."

I remember an incident where a "Palestinian" was throwing rocks at some Jews. The police, in an effort to quell the rioting, fired rubber bullets at the rock throwers to disperse them and halt their misbehavior. His wife, whom he had been hiding behind, got hit by one of those little projectiles resulting in a minor bruise. He was vowing to take revenge by killing as many Jews as he could, completely ignoring his own culpability in the whole incident. An appeal to him to exercise a bit of reasonableness or restraint fell on deaf ears and actually only seemed to agitate him further.

The law's, cited by Jesus, original intent was to discourage rigorous and bitter revenge but it had degenerated by Jesus' day to a base level, however, He not only brings it back to its original intent but elevates it further by saying that if we be insulted we ought to let it pass rather than rush off to court for redress of the wrong and bear any injury that can be borne for the sake of peace and commit the matter to the perfect magistrate, the Lord. Proverbs 20:22, "Say not thou, I will recompense evil; *but* wait on the LORD, and he shall save thee."

Jesus protested when smitten on the cheek (John_18:22). And Jesus denounced the Pharisees

(Matthew 23) and fought the devil always. The language of Jesus is bold and picturesque and is not to be pressed too literally. Paradoxes startle and make us think. We are expected to fill in the other side of the picture. One thing certainly is meant by Jesus and that is that personal revenge is taken out of our hands, and that applies to "lynch-law." Aggressive or offensive war by nations is also condemned, but not necessarily defensive war or defense against robbery and murder. Professional pacifism may be mere cowardice. – Robertson's Word Pictures

5:40 And if any man will sue thee at the law, and take away thy coat, let him have *thy* cloke also.

In America, in this present day, we tend not to know how onerous to the first hearers these statements were. They were being taught by some that they should not only get even, but that they should get ahead and Jesus claimed God never authorized that attitude.

After His explanation concerning right and wrong attitudes regarding the law, Jesus gives a number of examples. He introduces these examples with statements such as "You have heard it said." Clearly, this is not the same as "It is written." Jesus is not quoting from the Old Testament teachings but from the teachings of the Scribes and the Pharisees. He is not contradicting the law but the interpretations of the law that the Scribes taught. In the process of doing so He explains the real meaning of the law and the necessity for more than mere legal obedience. He is not giving or writing new law, rather He is showing the people that they must have a new attitude. The Jewish religious leaders used the law to govern outward actions, but Jesus wants the law to control the heart.

Besides controlling their anger, disciples of Jesus should try to make peace with those who are angry with them. Even in worldly affairs an offender would be wise to reach a settlement with his opponent quickly. Otherwise he may find himself in worse circumstances by receiving an unfavorable judgment in court.

5:41 And whosoever shall compel thee to go a mile, go with him twain.

An allusion, probably, to the practice of the Romans and some Eastern nations, who, when government dispatches had to be forwarded, obliged the people not only to furnish horses and carriages, but to give personal attendance, often at great inconvenience, when required. But the thing here demanded is a readiness to submit to unreasonable demands of whatever kind, rather than raise quarrels, with all the evils resulting from them. What follows is a beautiful extension of this precept. – Jamieson, Faussett, and Brown Commentary

5:42 Give to him that asketh thee, and from him that would borrow of thee turn not thou away.

5:43 Ye have heard that it hath been said, Thou shalt love thy neighbour, and hate thine enemy.

The saying that encouraged Jews to hate their enemies did not come from the law of Moses. God spoke the former part; the scribes added the latter. See Leviticus 19:48.

The people were being taught by their leadership that although they could not do injury to the Gentiles they were not to rescue them if they saw them in danger of death. Paul, in Romans 12:20, quotes Proverbs 25:22 to prove that we ought to treat our enemies kindly.

> 5:44 But I say unto you, Love your enemies, bless them that curse you, do good to them that hate you, and pray for them which despitefully use you, and persecute you;
> 5:45 That ye may be the children of your Father which is in heaven: for he maketh his sun to rise on the evil and on the good, and sendeth rain on the just and on the unjust.

The Christian's example is found in God, who gives rain and food to those who love Him as well as those who hate Him.

1st Peter 2:21-24; 3:9; Romans 12:20-21. Our incomparable interpreter of the law is telling us via this discourse the design of the law as intended from the very beginning; precepts that are only seen by correctly comprehending our Creator. As we better understand we are more capable of seeing the grace of God behind the law laid out in the Scripture.

The law of God, as laid out in the Old Testament, is actually designed to be beneficial to all men. The way Jesus elevates its function and intent is something that is truly only designed for those who are part of the kingdom of God; those outside of His kingdom are under no obligation to follow His commands because they are not His children. Now if God had not loved us while we were yet His enemies, we could never have become His children.

> 5:46 For if ye love them which love you, what reward have ye? do not even the publicans the same?
> 5:47 And if ye salute your brethren only, what do ye

more *than others?* do not even the publicans so?

5:48 Be ye therefore perfect, even as your Father which is in heaven is perfect.

I. What is not to be understood by this requirement, or what Christian perfection is not. Not perfection of knowledge, freedom from temptation, conflict, etc.

II. What is the perfection here required? Perfect obedience to the law of God.
III. That this perfection is a duty. For God requires it.
IV. That it is attainable. It is commanded-God wills it; it is promised; it is the object for which the Holy Spirit is promised and given, etc. – *Professor Finney.*

Be ye therefore perfect - as your Father - God himself is the grand law, sole giver, and only pattern of the perfection which he recommends to his children. The words are very emphatic, εσεσθε ουν υμεις τελειοι, Ye shall be therefore perfect - ye shall be filled with the spirit of that God whose name is Mercy, and whose nature is love. God has many imitators of his power, independence, justice, etc., but few of his love, condescension, and kindness. He calls himself Love, to teach us that in this consists that perfection, the attainment of which he has made both our duty and privilege: for these words of our Lord include both a command and a promise.

"Can we be fully saved from sin in this world?" is an important question, to which this text gives a satisfactory answer: "Ye shall be perfect, as your Father, who is in heaven, is perfect." - As in his infinite nature there is no sin, nothing but goodness and love, so in your finite nature there shall dwell no sin, for the law of the spirit of life in Christ Jesus shall make you free from the law of sin and death, Rom_8:2. God shall live in, fill, and rule your hearts; and, in what He fills and influences, neither Satan nor sin can have any part. If men, slighting their own mercies, cry out, "This is impossible!" - Whom does this arguing reprove - God, who, on this ground, has given a command, the fulfillment of which is impossible. "But who can bring a clean out of an unclean thing?" God Almighty - and, however inveterate the disease of sin may be, the grace of the Lord Jesus can fully cure it; and who will say, that he who laid down his life for our souls will not use his power completely to effect that salvation which he has died to procure. "But where is the person thus saved?" Wherever he is found who loves God with all his heart, soul, mind, and strength, and his neighbor as himself; and, for the honor of Christianity and its Author, may we not hope there are many such in the Church of God, not known indeed by any profession of this kind which they make, but by a surer testimony, that of uniformly holy tempers, piety to God, and beneficence to man? – Adam Clarke's Commentary

CHAPTER SIX

6:1 Take heed that ye do not your alms before men, to be seen of them: otherwise ye have no reward of your Father which is in heaven.

In the foregoing chapter our Lord particularly described the nature of inward holiness. In this he describes that purity of intention without which none of our outward actions are holy. It is not that others must not see but that if they are merely being done in order to be seen and admired, that is what our Lord condemns.

We are to let our light shine before men (Matthew 5:16) so that God would be glorified without our seeking to merely glorify ourselves. Psalm 106:3 "...Blessed is he that doeth righteousness at all times." Of course, if a person is not a follower of Christ Jesus then he absolutely should make sure everyone notices his alms-giving because he is <u>not</u> going to receive any reward from God.

6:2 Therefore when thou doest *thine* alms, do not sound a trumpet before thee, as the hypocrites do in the synagogues and in the streets, that they may have glory of men. Verily I say unto you, They have their reward.

The duty is not less necessary because some abuse it by making it serve their pride. However it does not necessarily follow that all good works done publicly forfeit God's approval; we are not to hide our light but we are to guard against wrong motivation.

> 6:3 But when thou doest alms, let not thy left hand know what thy right hand doeth:

Many times our works of charity must be hidden from even our nearest relatives, who, if they knew, would hinder us from doing what God has given the power and inclination to perform. At times we must go even farther by not thinking of them once done. They are given to God, and should be hidden in Him lest vain-glory creep in and make of thee a spoil.

> 6:4 That thine alms may be in secret: and thy Father which seeth in secret himself shall reward thee openly.

The right way to pray

> 6:5 And when thou prayest, thou shalt not be as the hypocrites *are:* for they love to pray standing in the synagogues and in the corners of the streets, that they may be seen of men. Verily I say unto you, They have their reward.

These were the usual places of prayer (synagogues) and the street corners where crowds stopped for business or talk. If the hour of prayer overtook a Pharisee here, he would strike his attitude of prayer like a modern Moslem that men might see that he was pious. – Robertson's Word Pictures

It is taken for granted that all they who are actual followers of The Christ pray. If one is prayerless then he is graceless for he is endeavoring to live independently of God and trusting in his own abilities whether inadvertently or advertently. Seven days without prayer makes one weak.

> 6:6 But thou, when thou prayest, enter into thy closet, and when thou hast shut thy door, pray to thy Father which is in secret; and thy Father which seeth in secret shall reward thee openly.

This does not discourage or forbid public prayer to lead others in prayer; rather it addresses the personal prayer which is a secret conversation of one heart with another which the world is too profane and treacherous to be a partaker thereof.

"The root that produces the beautiful and flourishing tree, with all its spreading branches, verdant leaves, and refreshing fruit, that which gains for it sap, life, vigor, and fruitfulness, is all unseen; and the farther and deeper the roots spread beneath, the more the tree expands above. Christians! if you wish to prosper, if you long to bring forth the fruits of the Spirit, strike your roots wide in private prayer." – *Salter.*

"As the tender dew that falls in the silent night makes the grass and herbs and flowers to flourish and grow more abundantly than great showers of rain that fall in the day, so secret prayer will more abundantly cause the sweet herbs of grace and holiness to grow and flourish in the soul, than all those more open, public and visible duties of religion, which too, too often are mingled and mixed with the sun and wind of pride and hypocrisy." – *Brooks*

6:7 But when ye pray, use not vain repetitions, as the heathen *do:* for they think that they shall be heard for their much speaking.

Prayer requires far more of the heart than of the tongue because it is a communication with a living, holy, God who hears and responds. The eloquence of prayer consists in the fervency of desire and the simplicity of faith. Unmeaning words, useless repetitions, and complimentary phrases in prayer, are in general the result of heathenism, hypocrisy, or ignorance.

I was once asked to close the worship service in prayer. The sermon had fully connected with me and I felt an uncustomary intensity of spirit within and prayed for merely a minute, or so I thought, it was over fifteen minutes in length. Our church's custom was general handshaking and bits of chatter as folk begin to leave following the closing prayer. The hand shaking occurred but all were quiet as they left the sanctuary that morning. It was at that point that I saw a clock and suddenly realized how long a prayer I had offered – I was so embarrassed!

That evening the Pastor ended his sermon a bit earlier than was his custom and asked me to once again close in prayer and that time it lasted only close to a minute in length. Following the prayer, folk were gathering around me and asking "What happened?" Much to my surprise, they were all hoping for a repeat of the morning's prayer. It had been intense and the Holy Spirit's presence had been felt by everyone, saint and sinner, young and old, and no one, absolutely no one in that worship service, had been aware of how much time had passed until after the fact. How wonderful it would be for us to pray like that each and every time.

This judicious note is from the late Mr. Gilbert Wakefield, who illustrates it with the following quotation from the Heautontimorumenos of Terence:

Ohe! jam decine Deos, uxor, gratulando Obtundere,
Tuam esse inventam gnatam: nisi illos ex Tuo Ingenio judicas,
Ut nil credas Intelligere, nisi idem Dictum Sit Centies

"Pray thee, wife, cease from Stunning the gods with thanksgivings, because thy child is in safety; unless thou judgest of them from thyself, that they cannot Understand a thing, unless they are told of it a Hundred Times." Heaut. ver. 880. – Adam Clarke

6:8 Be not ye therefore like unto them: for your Father knoweth what things ye have need of, before ye ask him.

Prayer is not designed to inform God, but to give man a sight of his misery; to humble his heart, to excite his desire, to inflame his faith, to animate his hope, to raise his soul from earth to heaven, and to put him in mind that There is his Father, his country, and inheritance. – Adam Clarke Commentary

6:9 After this manner therefore pray ye: Our Father which art in heaven, Hallowed be thy name.

After this manner therefore pray ye - Forms of prayer were frequent among the Jews; and every public teacher gave one to his disciples. Some forms were drawn out to a considerable length, and from these abridgments were made: to the latter sort the following prayer properly belongs, and consequently, besides its own very important use, it is a plan for a more extended devotion. What satisfaction must it be to learn from God himself, with what words, and in what manner, he would have us pray to him, so as not to pray in vain! A king, who draws up the petition which he allows to be presented to himself, has doubtless the fullest determination to grant the request. We do not sufficiently consider the value of this prayer; the respect and attention which it requires; the preference to be given to it; its fullness and perfection: the frequent use we should make of it; and the spirit which we should bring with it. "Lord, teach us how to pray!" is a prayer necessary to prayer; for unless we are divinely instructed in the manner, and influenced by the spirit of true devotion, even the prayer taught us by Jesus Christ may be repeated without profit to our souls.

Our Father - It was a maxim of the Jews, that a man should not pray alone, but join with the Church; by which they particularly meant that he should, whether alone or with the synagogue, use the plural number as comprehending all the followers of God. Hence, they say, Let none pray the short prayer, i.e. as the gloss expounds it, the prayer in the singular, but in the plural number. See Lightfoot on this place.

This prayer was evidently made in a peculiar manner for the children of God. And hence we are taught to say, not "My Father", but "Our Father".

The heart of a child of God, is a brotherly heart, in respect to all other Christians: it asks nothing but in the spirit of unity, fellowship, and Christian charity; desiring that for its brethren which it desires for itself.

The word Father, placed here at the beginning of this prayer, includes two grand ideas, which should serve as a foundation to all our petitions:

1st. That tender and respectful love which we should feel for God, such as that which children feel for their fathers.

2dly. That strong confidence in God's love to us, such as fathers have for their children.

Thus all the petitions in this prayer stand in strictest reference to the word "Father;" the first three referring to the love we have for God; and the three last, to that confidence which we have in the love He bears to us.

The relation we stand in to this first and best of beings dictates to us reverence for his person, zeal for his honor, obedience to his will, submission to his dispensations and chastisements, and resemblance to his nature.

Which art in heaven - The phrase אבינו שבשמים, abinu sheboshemayim, our Father who art in heaven, was very common among the ancient Jews; and was used by them precisely in the same sense as it is used here by our Lord.

This phrase in the Scriptures seems used to express:

1st. His Omnipresence. The heaven of heavens cannot contain thee. 1Ki_8:27 .

2dly. His Majesty and Dominion over his creatures. Art thou not God in heaven, and rulest thou not over all the kingdoms of the heathen? 2Ch_20:6.

3dly. His Power and Might. Art thou not God in heaven, and in thy hand is there not power and might, so that no creature is able to withstand thee! 2Ch_20:6. Our God is in heaven, and hath done whatsoever he pleased. Psa_115:3.

4thly. His Omniscience. The Lord's throne is in heaven, his eyes behold, his eye-lids try the children of men. Psa_11:4. The Lord looketh down from heaven, he beholdeth all the sons of men. Psa_33:13-15.

5thly. His infinite Purity and Holiness. Look down from thy holy habitation, etc. Deu_26:15. Thou art the high and lofty One, who inhabiteth eternity, whose name is holy. Isa_57:15.

Hallowed - Αγιασθητω. Αγιαζω· from α negative, and γη, the earth, a thing separated from the earth, or from earthly purposes and employments. As the word sanctified, or hallowed, in Scripture, is frequently used for the consecration of a thing or person to a holy use or office, as the Levites, first-born, tabernacle, temple, and their utensils, which were all set apart from every earthly, common, or profane use, and employed wholly in the service of God, so the Divine Majesty may be said to be sanctified by us, in analogy to those things, viz. when, we separate him from, and in our conceptions and desires exalt him above, earth and all things.

Thy name - That is, God himself, with all the attributes of his Divine nature - his power, wisdom, justice, mercy, etc.

We hallow God's name,

1st. With our lips, when all our conversation is holy, and we speak of those things which are meet to minister grace to the hearers.

2dly. In our thoughts, when we suppress every rising evil, and have our tempers regulated by his grace and Spirit.

3dly. In our lives, when we begin, continue, and end our works to his glory. If we have an eye to God in all we perform, then every act of our common employment will be an act of religious worship.

4thly. In our families, when we endeavor to bring up our children in the discipline and admonition or the Lord; instructing also our servants in the way of righteousness.

5thly. In a particular calling or business, when we separate the falsity, deception, and lying, commonly practised, from it; buying and selling as in the sight of the holy and just God. – Adam Clarke Commentary

6:10 Thy kingdom come. Thy will be done in earth, as *it is* in heaven.

Thy kingdom come - The ancient Jews scrupled not to say: He prays not at all, in whose prayers there is no mention of the kingdom of God. Hence, they were accustomed to say, "Let him cause his kingdom to reign, and his redemption to flourish: and let the Messiah speedily come and deliver his people."

The universal sway of the scepter of Christ: - God has promised that the kingdom of Christ shall be exalted above all kingdoms. Dan_7:14-27. That it shall overcome all others, and be at last the universal empire. Isa_9:7. Connect this with the explanation given of this phrase, Mat_3:2.

Thy will be done - This petition is properly added to the preceding; for when the kingdom of righteousness, peace, and joy, in the Holy Spirit, is established in the heart, there is then an ample provision made for the fulfillment of the Divine will.

The will of God is infinitely good, wise, and holy; to have it fulfilled in and among men, is to have infinite goodness, wisdom, and holiness diffused throughout the universe; and earth made the counterpart of heaven.

As it is in heaven - The Jews maintained, that they were the angels of God upon earth, as these pure spirits were angels of God in heaven; hence they said, "As the angels sanctify the Divine name in heaven, so the Israelites [/Christians are to] sanctify the Divine name, upon earth." See Schoettgen.

Observe,

1st. The salvation of the soul is the result of two wills conjoined: the will of God, and the will of man. If God will not do the salvation of man, he cannot be saved: If, man will not accept the salvation God has prepared for him, he cannot be delivered from his sins.

2dly. This petition certainly points out a deliverance from all sin; for nothing that is unholy can consist with the Divine will, and if this be fulfilled in man, surely sin shall be banished from his soul.

3dly. This is farther evident from these words, as it is in heaven; i.e. as the angels do it: viz. with all zeal, diligence, love, delight, and perseverance.

4thly. Does not the petition plainly imply, we may live without sinning against God? Surely the holy angels never mingle iniquity with their loving obedience; and as our Lord teaches us to pray, that we do his will here as they do it in heaven, can it be thought he would put a petition in our mouths, the fulfillment of which was impossible?

5thly. This certainly destroys the assertion: "There is no such state of purification, to be attained here, in which it may be said, the soul is redeemed from sinful passions and desires;" for it is on Earth that we are commanded to pray that this will, which is our sanctification, may be done.

6thly. Our souls can never be truly happy, till our Wills be entirely subjected to, and become one with, the will of God.

7thly. How can any person offer this petition to his Maker, who thinks of nothing less than the performance of the will of God, and of nothing more than doing his own?

Some see the mystery of the Trinity in the three preceding petitions. The first being, addressed to the Father, as the source of all holiness. The second, to the Son, who establishes the kingdom of God upon earth. The third, to the Holy Spirit, who by his energy works in men to will and to perform.

To offer these three petitions with success at the throne of God, three graces, essential to our salvation, must be brought into exercise; and, indeed, the petitions themselves necessarily suppose them.

Faith, Our Father - for he that cometh to God, must believe that he is.

Hope, Thy kingdom come - For this grace has for its object good things to come.

Love, Thy will be done - For love is the incentive to and principle of all obedience to God, and beneficence to man. – Adam Clarke Commentary

6:11 Give us this day our daily bread.

Give us this day our daily bread - The word επιουσιαν has greatly perplexed critics and commentators. I find upwards of thirty different explanations of it. It is found in no Greek writer before the evangelists, and Origen says expressly, that it was formed by them. The interpretation of Theophylact, one of the best of the Greek fathers, has ever appeared to me to be the most correct, Bread, sufficient for our substance and support, i.e. That quantity of food which is necessary to support our health and strength, by being changed into the substance of our bodies. ...There is probably an allusion here to the custom of travelers in the east, who were wont to reserve a part of the food given them the preceding evening to serve for their breakfast or dinner the next day. But as this was not sufficient for the whole day, they were therefore obliged to depend on the providence of God for the additional supply. In Luk_15:12, Luk_15:13, ουσια signifies, what a person has to live on; and nothing can be more natural than to understand the compound επιουσιος, of that additional supply which the traveler needs, to complete the provision necessary for a day's eating, over and above what he had then in his possession. See Harmer.

The word is so very peculiar and expressive, and seems to have been made on purpose by the evangelists, that more than mere bodily nourishment seems to be intended by it. Indeed, many of the primitive fathers understood it as comprehending that daily supply of grace which the soul requires to keep it in health and vigor: He who uses the petition would do well to keep both in view. Observe

1. God is the author and dispenser of all temporal as well as spiritual good.

2. We have merited no kind of good from his hand, and therefore must receive it as a free gift: Give us, etc.

3. We must depend on him daily for support; we are not permitted to ask any thing for to-morrow: give us to-day.

4. That petition of the ancient Jews is excellent: "Lord, the necessities of thy people Israel are many, and their knowledge small, so that they know not how to disclose their necessities: Let it be thy good pleasure to give to every man, what sufficeth for food!" Thus they expressed their dependence, and left it to God to determine what was best and most suitable.

We must ask only that which is essential to our support, God having promised neither luxuries nor superfluities. – Adam Clarke

6:12 And forgive us our debts, as we forgive our debtors.

And forgive us our debts - Sin is represented here under the notion of a debt, and as our sins are many, they are called here debts. God made man that he might live to his glory, and gave him a law to walk by; and if, when he does any thing that tends not to glorify God, he contracts a debt with Divine Justice, how much more is he debtor when he breaks the law by actual transgression! It has been justly observed, "All the attributes of God are reasons of obedience to man; those attributes are infinite; every sin is an act of ingratitude or rebellion against all these attributes; therefore sin is infinitely sinful."

Forgive us - Man has nothing with which to pay: if his debts are not forgiven, they must stand charged against him forever, as he is absolutely insolvent. Forgiveness, therefore, must come from the free mercy of God in Christ: and how strange is it we cannot have the old debt canceled, without (by that very means) contracting a new one, as great as the old! but the credit is transferred from Justice to Mercy. While sinners we are in debt to infinite Justice; when pardoned, in debt to endless Mercy: and as a continuance in a state of grace necessarily implies a continual communication of mercy, so the debt goes on increasing ad infinitum. Strange economy in the Divine procedure, which by rendering a man an infinite debtor, keeps him eternally dependent on his Creator! How good is God! And what does this state of dependence imply? A union with, and participation of, the fountain of eternal goodness and felicity!

As we forgive our debtors - It was a maxim among the ancient Jews, that no man should lie down in his bed, without forgiving those who had offended him. That man condemns himself to suffer eternal punishment, who makes use of this prayer with revenge and hatred in his heart. He who will not attend to a condition so advantageous to himself (remitting a hundred pence to his debtor, that his own creditor may remit him 10,000 talents) is a madman, who, to oblige his neighbor to suffer an hour, is himself determined to suffer everlastingly! This condition of forgiving our neighbor, though it cannot possibly merit anything, yet it is that condition without which God will pardon no man. See Mat_6:14, Mat_6:15. – Adam Clarke

6:13 And lead us not into temptation, but deliver us from evil: For thine is the kingdom, and the power, and the glory, for ever. Amen.

And lead us not into temptation - That is, bring us not in to sore trial. Πειρασμον, which may be here rendered sore trial, comes from περω, to pierce through, as with a spear, or spit, used so by some of the best Greek writers. Several of the primitive fathers understood it something in this way; and have therefore added *quam ferre non possumus*, "which we cannot bear." The word not only implies violent assaults from Satan, but also sorely afflictive circumstances, none of which we have, as yet, grace or fortitude sufficient to bear. Bring us not in, or lead us not in. This is a mere Hebraism: God is said to do a thing which he only permits or suffers to be done.

The process of temptation is often as follows:

1st. A simple evil thought.

2ndly. A strong imagination, or impression made on the imagination, by the thing to which we are tempted.

3dly. Delight in viewing it.

4thly. Consent of the will to perform it. Thus lust is conceived, sin is finished, and death brought forth. Jam_1:15.

See also on Mat_4:1 (note). A man may be tempted without entering into the temptation: entering into it implies giving way, closing in with, and embracing it.

But deliver us from evil - from the wicked one. Satan is expressly called the wicked one, Mat_13:19, Mat_13:38, compare with Mar_4:15; Luk_8:12. This epithet of Satan comes from πονος, labor, sorrow, misery, because of the drudgery which is found in the way of sin, the sorrow that accompanies the commission of it, and the misery which is entailed upon it, and in which it ends.

It is said in the Mishna, Titus. Beracoth, that Rabbi Judah was wont to pray thus: "Let it be thy good pleasure to deliver us from impudent men, and from impudence: from an evil man and an evil chance; from an evil affection, an evil companion, and an evil neighbor: from Satan the destroyer, from a hard judgment, and a hard adversary." See Lightfoot.

Deliver us - Ρυσαι ημας - a very expressive word - break our chains, and loose our bands - snatch, pluck us from the evil, and its calamitous issue.

For thine is the kingdom, etc. - The whole of this doxology is rejected by Wetstein, Griesbach, and the most eminent critics. The authorities on which it is rejected may be seen in Griesbach and, Wetstein, particularly in the second edition of Griesbach's Testament, who is fully of opinion that it never made a part of the sacred text. It is variously written in several MSS., and omitted by most of the fathers, both Greek and Latin. As the doxology is at least very ancient, and was in use among the Jews, as well as all the other petitions of this excellent prayer, it should not, in my opinion, be left out of the text, merely because some MSS. have omitted it, and it has been variously written in others. See various forms of this doxology, taken from the ancient Jewish writers, in Lightfoot and Schoettgen.

By the kingdom, we may understand that mentioned Mat_6:10, and explained Mat_3:2.

By power, that energy by which the kingdom is governed and maintained.

By glory, the honor that shall redound to God in consequence of the maintenance of the kingdom of grace, in the salvation of men.

For ever and ever - to the for evers. Well expressed by our common translation - ever in our ancient use of the word taking in the whole duration of time; the second ever, the whole of eternity. May thy name have the glory both in this world, and in that which is to come! The original word αιων comes from αει always, and ων being, or existence. This is Aristotle's definition of it. See the note on Gen_21:33. There is no word in any language which more forcibly points out the grand characteristic of eternity - that which always exists. It is often used to signify a limited time, the end of which is not known; but this use of it is only an accommodated one; and it is the grammatical and proper sense of it which must be resorted to in any controversy concerning the word. We sometimes use the phrase for evermore: i.e. for ever and more, which signifies the whole of time, and the more or interminable duration beyond it. See on Mat_25:46 (note).

Amen - This word is Hebrew, אמן, and signifies faithful or true. Some suppose the word is formed from the initial letters of אדוני מלך נאם adoni melech neetnan, My Lord, the faithful King. The word itself implies a confident resting of the soul in God, with the fullest assurance that all these petitions shall be fulfilled to everyone who prays according to the directions given before by our blessed Lord. – Adam Clarke

6:14 For if ye forgive men their trespasses, your heavenly Father will also forgive you:
6:15 But if ye forgive not men their trespasses, neither will your Father forgive your trespasses.

The right way to fast

6:16 Moreover when ye fast, be not, as the hypocrites, of a sad countenance: for they disfigure their faces, that they may appear unto men to fast. Verily I say unto you, They have their reward.

The term means "eat not" or total abstinence from food for a certain period of time. Abstaining from meat and living on fish, vegetables, etc., is not a fast, or should only be considered a parody of fasting.

The hypocrite, or pretender, tries to appear to have godly sorrow and he counterfeits it as best as he can which usually manifests outwardly as a gloomy and austere look. Sincere fasting frequently may manifest itself in one failing to take care of the external appearance which is not a problem if one is able to remain secluded in their prayer-closet for the duration. However Jesus says, in effect, comb your hair, wash your face and smile if you're going to be seen by others so that no one, but you and God has any reason to suspect that you are fasting.

A rather peculiar form of "fasting" has emerged in these days which is probably best described as "tag-team fasting" wherein one person fasts for a few hours then someone else takes up the fast for a few hours. That particular style seems to usually be attached to rather dubious causes by folks of questionable character, anyway

> 6:17 But thou, when thou fastest, anoint thine head, and wash thy face;
>
> 6:18 That thou appear not unto men to fast, but unto thy Father which is in secret: and thy Father, which seeth in secret, shall reward thee openly.

Thy Father which seeth – "Let us not be afraid that our hearts can be concealed from God; but let us fear lest He perceive them to be more desirous of praise of men than they are of that glory which comes from Him." – Adam Clarke

> 6:19 Lay not up for yourselves treasures upon earth, where moth and rust doth corrupt, and where thieves

break through and steal:

The dangers of riches are often mentioned in the NT but nowhere are they condemned in and of themselves. What Jesus condemns here is greed and hoarding of money. *Moth and rust* are representative of all agents and processes that destroy worldly possessions.

It has been said: "No man ever went to heaven whose heart was not there before." You can't take it with you but you can send it ahead. Here all things are perishable and passing there all thing are pure and permanent. Worldly-mindedness is a common and fatal symptom among men. Christ counsels to keep our confidence in the joys and glories of the other world which is eternal. Everything done for God's grace and glory is like something planted in the eternal world and while it may seem to disappear now it will appear again.

A Christian may lay up treasures in Heaven by:

1. Selecting for our friends and companions those who are children of God, so that each departing one is an actual increase of the holy treasure which is awaiting us over there.
2. Seeking and befriending some who are not yet children of God and guiding them to becoming part of God's forever family. Such ones as they are the more valuable treasure for over there.

Have a deposit on earth, if you must or can; but let your chief banking be in Heaven. – H. W. Beecher

6:20 But lay up for yourselves treasures in heaven, where neither moth nor rust doth corrupt, and where thieves do not break through nor steal:

6:21 For where your treasure is, there will your heart be also.

An earthly minded man proves that his treasure is here below but a heavenly minded man shows that his treasure is above. There is no real need to worry about becoming "so Heavenly minded that you are of no earthly good." That is a canard that is cast on occasion by earthly minded ones calculated to confuse the situation and weaken the effect of your testimony.

6:22 The light of the body is the eye: if therefore thine eye be single, thy whole body shall be full of light.

See Proverbs 4:25-27

Or, in other words, being able to see clearly and correctly. Many men seem to maliciously and wickedly put out the little bit of light that is within them and then, not being content to wallow in their own darkness, they then attempt to extinguish the light that others have.

> The eye is the lamp of the body – and what the eye is to the body, the intention is to the soul. Fix your eye on God and Heaven and your whole soul will be full of holiness and happiness.

The "eye" is "single," not because it sees *one thing,* but because it looks in *one direction.* It is a simplicity, not of the *intellectual,* but of the *moral* regards. It marks one ruling passion to which all others are pressed into subservience. A navigator may set his mind on the discovery of some distant region, and may repel all the temptations he meets with in his way; not allowing the luxury of one place, or the gain of another, to detain him. Here is singleness of eye; but yet he attends to the waters below, and to the firmament above, and to the compass by which he steers his course. Here the object is one, but its pursuit is illuminated by the light of many sciences. (*Dr. Chalmers*)

6:23 But if thine eye be evil, thy whole body shall be full of darkness. If therefore the light that is in thee be darkness, how great *is* that darkness!

If the "light" within us be darkness, how awful, how mischievous is that darkness! An evil eye was a phrase, among ancient Jews that denoted an envious covetous person or disposition; a person who fretted at his neighbor's, real or imagined, prosperity, loved his own money so much so that he would no nothing in the way of charity personally but expected others to be expending their, obviously hoarded, maybe even ill-gotten, goods for charitable purposes. The similarity to the American Democrats being purely and completely coincidental, or not.

To be in a room with great pictures and not be able to see them is grief; to be in a world filled with expressions of the creator's love and power, and not to see them is an unutterable tragedy. Thus the greatest misery and misfortune that can befall us is to have our conscious depraved and corrupted. If the light within be darkness, how awful....

6:24 No man can serve two masters: for either he will hate the one, and love the other; or else he will hold to the one, and despise the other. Ye cannot serve God and mammon.

Neutrality in religion is exposed here. Some contrive to elude the truth of this maxim but those efforts merely render the general truth all the more remarkable.

Mammon may actually be anything a person places his confidence in, usually considered to be riches because of the influence they tend to wield.

> I believe that it is anti-Christian and unholy for any Christian to live with the object of accumulating wealth. You will say, "Are we not to strive all we can to get all the money we can?" You may do so. I cannot doubt but what, in so doing, you may do service to the cause of God. But what I said was that to live with the object of accumulating wealth is anti-Christian. - Tom Carted, ed., 2,200 Quotations from the Writings of Charles H. Spurgeon (Grand Rapids: Baker Book House, 1988), 216.

The man who truly serves his master serves him with singleness of heart, with a mind wholly given to his service. Two motives weigh with a man in selecting masters, interest or gratitude. Jesus shows here the utter impossibility of loving the world and loving God at the same time; or, in other words, that a man of the world cannot be truly Christian in character. God can do more for you than mammon can. God claims your service on the ground of what He has done for you. A person may appear to serve both for a time but as soon as contrary interests arise it will be seen quite clearly to which he really belongs.

He who gives his heart to the world robs God of it, and in the snatching at the passing shadow of earthly goods, loses substantial and eternal blessings. How dangerous it is to set our hearts upon riches, seeing it is so easy to make them our god.

The service to Christianity does not demand greater privations than that of sin. God's designs in employing us in His service are to our benefit, not His need. God asks for our time, mammon takes it.

> 6:25 Therefore I say unto you, Take no thought for your life, what ye shall eat, or what ye shall drink; nor yet for your body, what ye shall put on. Is not the life more than meat, and the body than raiment?

The Christian should live in quiet confidence in God. Undue anxiety is reproved herein. Anxiety distorts the future. Prudent care is not forbidden by our Lord. To be anxiously careful concerning the means of subsistence is to lose all satisfaction and comfort in the things God gives, and to act like a mere infidel. On the other hand, to rely so much on providence as to not use the very powers and faculties which He has endowed us with is to tempt God.

When we commit our whole temporal condition to the wit of our own minds then we get into that "unsettled" state against which our Lord exhorts His followers. Additionally, the command can also mean that we are to stop such worrying if we are already engaging in it. Therefore we are to beware of over engaging in worldly cares; for these are as inconsistent with the true service to God and our fellow man. If God give the greater gift will He deny the smaller?

> 6:26 Behold the fowls of the air: for they sow not, neither do they reap, nor gather into barns; yet your heavenly Father feedeth them. Are ye not much better than they?

The second reason we should not be overly anxious about the future. This, of course does not mean that men should not sow or reap or gather into barns for even the birds are diligent in their own way. But we should never forget that we do have a heavenly Father who does care about our well-being.

6:27 Which of you by taking thought can add one cubit unto his stature?

6:28 And why take ye thought for raiment? Consider the lilies of the field, how they grow; they toil not, neither do they spin:

6:29 And yet I say unto you, That even Solomon in all his glory was not arrayed like one of these.

6:30 Wherefore, if God so clothe the grass of the field, which today is, and tomorrow is cast into the oven, *shall he* not much more *clothe* you, O ye of little faith?

6:31 Therefore take no thought, saying, What shall we eat? or, What shall we drink? or, Wherewithal shall we be clothed?

6:32 (For after all these things do the Gentiles seek:) for your heavenly Father knoweth that ye have need of all these things.

6:33 But seek ye first the kingdom of God, and his righteousness; and all these things shall be added unto you.

That holiness of heart and life which God requires of those that profess to be part of His spiritual kingdom. Failure to be, refusal to be, holy is bearing His name in vain. Grace is the way to glory; holiness the way to happiness. If men be not righteous there is no heave to be had (Matthew 5:20): if they be, they shall have heaven and earth as well; for godliness has the promise of both lives (1st Timothy 6:3-8; John 15:11, 14:23-24).

Men who hate the Lord Jesus the Christ will hate us and seek to interfere with the blessings our Lord would bestow upon His children but, even if they succeed, that is not detrimental to our heavenly abode which they have no part in.

6:34 Take therefore no thought for the morrow: for the morrow shall take thought for the things of itself. Sufficient unto the day *is* the evil thereof.

CHAPTER SEVEN

7:1 Judge not, that ye be not judged.

These verses involve some of the most delicate and vital duties of the Christian life. Many people tend to treat them rather superficially as though only the first verse exists, "Somewhere in the Bible," and the rest of the verses which explain what our Lord intended aren't there at all. Unfortunately it is also among the most misused and abused of exhortations, especially by hypocrites seeking to silence the voices of those who may be accurately touching upon a character flaw they posses. When a person starts squawking like a demented parrot, "Judge not, judge not," then it is fairly apparent that there is some truth to the accusation that may or may not have been leveled.

The prohibition from our Lord refers primarily to the conduct of private individuals, not to those serving in a public capacity; however it is not intended to hinder private persons from forming an opinion based upon the misconduct of others. These exhortations are pointed against rash, harsh, and uncharitable judgments, the thinking evil, where no evil seems, and speaking of it accordingly. We are expected to reform our own conduct and ensure we are ourselves walking in all of the light available to us so that we may judge in a proper manner. The Jews were highly criminal in this regard, yet they had very excellent maxims against it.

By a secretive and criminal disposition of nature, man tends to endeavor to elevate himself above others, and, sometimes, to see them elevated, depresses him. His jealous and envious heart wishes that there may be no good quality found in any but himself, that he alone may be esteemed above all others. Such is the state of nearly every unconverted man and even many who call themselves Christian; it is from this criminal disposition, that evil surmises, rash judgments, and all other unjust procedures against our neighbor flow.

It is not that Christians are not to judge but they are not to judge hypocritically or self-righteously, as can be seen from the context of this section of the sermon. The world's opinion does not matter because it does not accurately comprehend things of God. We Christ followers are to so put on the mind and character of The Christ so that as we make necessary judgments we have an assurance that He would not disapprove.

All Christians are called to do the Great Commission and those who present the gospel must be able to judge the difference between people who genuinely want to know about God and people who only want to mock and abuse. That is not always easy to discern. The followers of Jesus must therefore learn to make proper judgments if they are to help others. As teachers and disciple makers they are examples, and God will reward them according to the example they give, whether good or bad. They must remember that they cannot lead the blind if they themselves are blind.

> 7:2 For with what judgment ye judge, ye shall be judged: and with what measure ye mete, it shall be measured to you again.

We are warned against judgments that are uncalled for. Sometimes it is our duty to judge as Christians. Now it is quite naturally true that the one who is severe on others will naturally excite their severity against himself. Therefore we want to avoid forming poorly defined and romantic notions of absolute human perfection in anything. For these are much more likely to heighten our expectations from others, and our demands upon them, than to increase our watchfulness over ourselves; and so every failure provokes us more than it otherwise might have done.

> 7:3 And why beholdest thou the mote that is in thy brother's eye, but considerest not the beam that is in thine own eye?

> Before thou reprehend another, take heed that thou art not culpable in what thou goest about to reprehend. He that cleanses a blot with blurred fingers will make a greater blot. Even the candle-snuffers of the sanctuary were of pure gold. – Quarles

When we shall have as much zeal to correct ourselves, as we have inclination to reprove and correct others, we shall know our own defects better than we now know those of our neighbor.

The minister, whose God-given task it is to declare to the people their faults and sins, should closely examine himself, lest, after he has preached to others, he himself should be cast-away.

A person who does not strive to keep sin out of his life cannot be a good counselor or bold reprover; such a one must speak softly for fear of awakening his own guilty conscience.

> 7:4 Or how wilt thou say to thy brother, Let me pull out the mote out of thine eye; and, behold, a beam *is* in thine own eye?

That man is utterly unfit to show the way of life to others who is himself walking in the way of death.

> 7:5 Thou hypocrite, first cast out the beam out of thine own eye; and then shalt thou see clearly to cast out the mote out of thy brother's eye.

Our Lord unmasks the vile pretender to saintship, and declares that his hidden hypocrisy, covered with the garb of external, imputed, sanctity, is more abominable in the sight of God than the openly professed and practiced iniquity of the profligate. "Cast out the little sin that is in thy hand: to which he answered, cast out the great sin that is in thine. So they could not reprove, because all were sinners." – Lightfoot

Thus we see how great a calamity cast upon Christendom by Calvin because he revived that antinomian spirit that said we all sin all the time because we are only a sinner saved by grace and we can never grow beyond that low level of spirituality this side of heaven. Folks who are content to walk in that path are, at best, "foolish ones" because Jesus said "Sin not," and He knows full well how to help us live blameless before God.

> 7:6 Give not that which is holy unto the dogs, neither cast ye your pearls before swine, lest they trample them

under their feet, and turn again and rend you.

We know that sacred things are liable to be abused by profane persons. It should really come as no surprise, then, when they use and misuse the sacred text to attack those who attempt to closely follow the ways of The Christ in order to inflict pain regarding perceived shortcomings or intimidate us into being silent at the very time when we should not be.

7:7 Ask, and it shall be given you; seek, and ye shall find; knock, and it shall be opened unto you:

Rogation Days are days of prayer and fasting from Monday to Wednesday preceding Ascension Thursday. The term comes from the Latin verb *Rogare* which means "to ask." Farmers often had their fields and crops blessed by a priest at this time.

> In May almost always the Rogation Days come. . . . These days are meant to prepare the people's hearts for the coming festival of the Ascension; but mainly to be days of intercession " for the fruits of the earth, which are then tender, that they may not be blasted," as well as for health and peace at that season of the year when war and pestilence may be expected to begin....
>
> We pray for a blessing upon the fruits of the earth. We can scarcely help it unless we are untrue to nature. Man's heart is on his fields; he has done all his work as far as crops are concerned-now he can only hope, watch, and pray. Now all depends upon what God will be pleased to do. We are not powerless: prayer is left to us. Thirteen centuries ago Rogation Days were first appointed; it was then felt that prayer was a power to secure peace and plenty. Though there is no *service* for

these Days, there is nothing to prevent us from keeping them. Our great authority for them is found in the first and second chapters of Joel. – *E. T. Marshall, M. A.*

In these days of greatly improved irrigation and farming techniques those days of prayer have mostly gone by the wayside, which is a shame. We need more prayer, not less.

7:8 For every one that asketh receiveth; and he that seeketh findeth; and to him that knocketh it shall be opened.

Prayer is the appointed means for obtaining what we need. Ask, as a beggar asks for alms. Seek, as for a thing of value that we have lost. Sin has set a barrier, a door which we have no capability to open between us and our Lord but He bids us knock.

7:9 Or what man is there of you, whom if his son ask bread, will he give him a stone?

7:10 Or if he ask a fish, will he give him a serpent?

7:11 If ye then, being evil, know how to give good gifts unto your children, how much more shall your Father which is in heaven give good things to them that ask him?

If ye, then, being evil - who are radically and diabolically depraved, yet feel yourselves led, by natural affection, to give those things to your children which are necessary to support their lives, how much more will your Father who is in heaven, whose nature is infinite goodness, mercy, and grace, give good things - his grace and Spirit (πνευμα αγιον), the Holy [Spirit], Luk_11:13), to them who ask him? What a picture is here given of the goodness of God! Reader, ask thy soul, could this heavenly Father reprobate to unconditional eternal damnation any creature he has made? He who can believe that he has, may believe anything: but still God Is Love. – Adam Clarke

That love is not the touchy-feely, Santa in the sky stuff, but perfect love such as seems beyond the comprehension of too many people in our day.

Now we arrive at a transitional point in this sermon. Heretofore He has laid out the doctrinal position and now begins the exhortation to put it all into practice.

> 7:12 Therefore all things whatsoever ye would that men should do to you, do ye even so to them: for this is the law and the prophets.

This is found in negative form in rabbinic Judaism and also in Hinduism, Buddhism, Confucianism, and in Greek and Roman ethical teaching. Thereby some have sought to downplay Jesus' statement here while missing the fact that He stated it in positive form; Christian righteousness is found in doing good, not just avoiding evil. Therefore, it can be argued that that this rule is expressed by no one else for though it might seem similar it is quite dissimilar to what others have tried to say and teach.

Barack Hussein Obama, shortly after assuming the office of the presidency in 2009, whined about the U.S. Constitution calling it a "Charter of negative liberties." To the average American that made no sense whatsoever because we view it, the Constitution, as a positive thing because it is a device designed to protect us from an overreaching government or any that would attempt to become a dictator. Much pain and suffering could have been avoided if we had paid attention and acted appropriately.

> "This is the substance of all relative duty; all Scripture in a nutshell." Incomparable summary! How well called "the royal law!" (Jam_2:8; compare Rom_13:9). It is true that similar maxims are found floating in the writings of the cultivated Greeks and Romans, and naturally enough in the Rabbinical writings. But so expressed as it is here - in immediate connection with, and as the sum of *such* duties as has been just enjoined, and such principles as had been before taught - it is to be found nowhere else. And the best commentary upon this fact is, that never till our Lord came down thus to teach did men effectually and widely exemplify it in their practice. The precise sense of the maxim is best referred to common sense. It is not, of course, what - in our wayward, capricious, gasping moods - we should *wish* that men would do to us, that we are to hold ourselves bound to do to them; but only what - in the exercise of an impartial judgment, and putting ourselves in their place - we consider it reasonable that they should do to us, that we are to do to them. – Jamieson, Fausset, and Brown Commentary

> 7:13 Enter ye in at the strait gate: for wide *is* the gate, and broad *is* the way, that leadeth to destruction, and many there be which go in thereat:

Vincent quotes the *Pinax* or *Tablet* of Cebes, a disciple of Socrates: "Seest thou not a little door, and a path before the door, which is not much frequented, only a few ascend it? That is the way that leadeth unto true culture." The tablet of Cebes is also known as "The Greek Pilgrim's progress" and was most likely actually written after Chrysostom but before Lucian (first half of second century AD) there being no proof of its existence prior to that time.

> 7:14 Because strait *is* the gate, and narrow *is* the way, which leadeth unto life, and few there be that find it.

True discipleship is a minority religion even among those who claim to be Christian. There are those who are foolish and there are they who are wise, and the dividing line between them is not always clear. Life – eternal life; it is not found by following the crowds, but by a deliberate decision to live the way of The Christ. It is not merely a matter of knowing and saying, but also of the doing, in other words, being like The Christ in thought, word, and deed.

> 7:15 Beware of false prophets, which come to you in sheep's clothing, but inwardly they are ravening wolves.

In the early New Testament church, prophesy was an honored gift but it fell into disfavor due the proliferation of the false prophets. One reason why many do not follow the narrow way is that they are deceived by those who teach their own views, often with ulterior motives, on how people can find meaning in life. Their teaching at first sounds sound and may show some temporary gains, but in the end it proves to be destructive. Those teachers appear to be as harmless as sheep but actually they are as dangerous as wolves preying on people instead of praying for them.

The Didache informs us that before the end of the first century false prophets were a serious problem. The connection of thought with verses 13-14 is that, like the false prophets in the Old Testament they would offer an easier alternative to the narrow way of Christian discipleship. As an example, there are the antinomians, which includes the "Positive Mental Attitude" (Prosperity Gospel) as well as the "I sin daily in thought, word, and deed" but-that-is-not-a-problem people. Yes, grace, absolutely, but we have also been called to purity. See Matthew 5:8.

> 7:16 Ye shall know them by their fruits. Do men gather grapes of thorns, or figs of thistles?

This truth gets repeated frequently because our eternal interests depend so much upon it. Not to have good fruit is to have bad; there can be no innocent sterility in the invisible tree of the heart. Our Lord makes it clear that he that brings forth bad fruit and he that brings forth no fruit are both fit only for the fire.

> 7:17 Even so every good tree bringeth forth good fruit; but a corrupt tree bringeth forth evil fruit.

Jesus sets an ethical test rather than a doctrinal test in this discourse.

But who expect to gather grapes of thorns and figs of thistles?
I. The man who expects to obtain happiness without a holy life.
II. The man who expects to obtain a holy life without a renewed heart.
III. The man who expects to obtain a renewed heart without faith in evangelical truth. (*R. Halley, D. D.*)

> 7:18 A good tree cannot bring forth evil fruit, neither *can* a corrupt tree bring forth good fruit.

> 7:19 Every tree that bringeth not forth good fruit is

hewn down, and cast into the fire.

Jesus here reinforces John the baptizer's attack on superficial repentance. This Gospel frequently emphasizes the danger of a purely nominal discipleship and warns that there will be professed Christians who will be rejected at the end because they remained in the camp of the "foolish virgins".

What a terrible proclamation this is against Christless hearers and Christless Pastors. Every impenitent person stands at the brink of eternal destruction.

7:20 Wherefore by their fruits ye shall know them.

Fruits, in the Scripture and Jewish phraseology, are taken for works of any kind. "A man's works," says one, "are the tongue of his heart, and tell honestly whether he is inwardly corrupt or pure."... The judgment formed of a man by his general conduct is a safe one: if the judgment be not favorable to the person, that is his fault, as you have your opinion of him from his works, i.e. the confession of his own heart. – Adam Clarke

Not by our acquired knowledge, or fancied experience, or creed; but by fruits. What one flavor should there be in all fruits? Many different flavors in fruits, yet there is something common to them which makes us approve of them all. we can call all fruit good, if we can detect in them the flavor of *godliness*-Christlikeness.   Therefore, unselfishness, thoughtfulness, truthfulness, gentleness. These flavors are to be found in our *words* and in our deeds.

1. The false prophets whom our Lord condemns were guilty of lowering the standard of moral duty by explaining away the spirituality and extent of the law, and reducing the whole of human obedience to a few technically unimportant ceremonies.

2. They frustrate the free grace of the gospel by insisting on the meritoriousness of human obedience. That is what the Judaising teachers in Corinth, Galatia, and Ephesus were doing.

> **The Christian, fruitful in a barren scene**
> Those who travel through deserts would often be at a loss for water, if certain indications, which the hand of Providence has marked out, did not serve to guide them to a supply. The secret wells are for the most part discoverable from the verdure which is nourished by their presence. So the fruitfulness of good works of the believer, amidst the deadness and sterility around him, proclaim the Christian's life. (*Salter.*)

> 7:21 Not every one that saith unto me, Lord, Lord, shall enter into the kingdom of heaven; but he that doeth the will of my Father which is in heaven.

There is a sharp contrast drawn between the mere talker and the doer of God's will. The first hearers of this sermon understood Jesus to be saying "No one who merely calls Me Lord will be allowed into Heaven."

> The sense of this verse seems to be this: No person, by merely acknowledging my authority, believing in the Divinity of my nature, professing faith in the perfection of my righteousness, and infinite merit of my atonement, shall enter into the kingdom of heaven - shall have any part with God in glory; but he who doeth the will of my Father - he who gets the bad tree rooted up, the good tree planted, and continues to bring forth

fruit to the glory and praise of God. –Adam Clarke

7:22 Many will say to me in that day, Lord, Lord, have we not prophesied in thy name? and in thy name have cast out devils? and in thy name done many wonderful works?

Ephesians 2:8-10 – Don't attempt to drop the tenth verse of this as many do In their Scripture memorization nor make it stand by itself as some others do for that passage says what Jesus is saying here. See also 2nd Timothy 2:19

7:23 And then will I profess unto them, I never knew you: depart from me, ye that work iniquity.

Merely saying that you are a believer in Jesus but not living like a true disciple of Jesus means you are not one of His followers and therefore, at best, you are numbered among the "five foolish" and will not gain entry into Heaven.

7:24 Therefore whosoever heareth these sayings of mine, and doeth them, I will liken him unto a wise man, which built his house upon a rock:

7:25 And the rain descended, and the floods came, and the winds blew, and beat upon that house; and it fell not: for it was founded upon a rock.

7:26 And every one that heareth these sayings of mine, and doeth them not, shall be likened unto a foolish man, which built his house upon the sand:

7:27 And the rain descended, and the floods came, and the winds blew, and beat upon that house; and it fell: and great was the fall of it.

7:28 And it came to pass, when Jesus had ended these sayings, the people were astonished at his doctrine:

7:29 For he taught them as *one* having authority, and not as the scribes.

The scribes could only repeat the regulations of Judaism and the opinions of respected teachers of the past. If they had stayed true to the teaching of the Torah instead of wandering off into the traditions of men they could have done a much better job of representing the will of God. Jesus cared very little for the traditions of men, especially those which had missed the point and gone astray from the intent of the law.

Jesus interpreted the law with an authority that came from God; it could even be argued that He was the one who gave them the law.

CHAPTER EIGHT

This and the next chapter concentrate on Jesus' healing ministry. Now that His authority has been established through His teaching ministry He demonstrates His authority through deed.

8:1 When he was come down from the mountain, great multitudes followed him.

Those who have been impressed by the authority of Jesus' words are now to be witnesses of His deeds.

8:2 And, behold, there came a leper and worshipped him, saying, Lord, if thou wilt, thou canst make me clean.

While other diseases are "healed" in the New Testament a leper is "cleansed" and it is the religious authorities who must certify this has taken place.

The "testimony" of these miracles is both negative and positive; a witness against those who reject Jesus; a call to belief in the holy one of God.

8:3 And Jesus put forth *his* hand, and touched him, saying, I will; be thou clean. And immediately his leprosy was cleansed.

8:4 And Jesus saith unto him, See thou tell no man; but go thy way, shew thyself to the priest, and offer the gift that Moses commanded, for a testimony unto them.

In the New Testament there is no disease regarded with more terror and pity than leprosy. When Jesus sent out the Twelve he commanded them "Heal the sick, cleanse lepers." (Matt 18:8) The fate of the leper was truly hard. There were some other skin diseases which were mistakenly classified as leprosy such as ringworm or psoriasis and when they went away there was a prescribed ritual to go through to be declared "clean."

It was a rule of law that the leprous person could not come closer than a stone's throw to a non-leprous person and if they did people would typically react in fear and drive them back with stones. From this record, on the surface, it appears the leper came closer than allowed but it is also more than likely that he actually did not, only coming as close as he legally could before falling to his knees and making his plea. Whether he came closer than allowed by law or stopped short isn't important; what is important is that Jesus cared enough to reach out and tenderly touch the untouchable one as well as completely cure. It was a demonstration of His Father's compassion; if we will only approach and plead He will bridge whatever gap remains because He longs to establish/restore the fellowship that has been broken by the barrier of sin between an unholy being and the thrice Holy God.

Many a man on the face of this planet ignorantly and

arrogantly thinks he will be able to approach God and plead the case that he himself is not so bad as some of his fellows and for that reason alone he must be allowed into heaven. Sadly, he will be met with justice rather than mercy because he has chosen to act in pride rather than humility. However, those who by faith apply to The Christ Jesus for mercy and grace will find that He is quite capable and willing to provide the mercy and the grace they need and seek but today is the day of salvation, tomorrow may be too late.

Jesus then sent the man to go fulfill the prescribed ritual.

8:5 And when Jesus was entered into Capernaum, there came unto him a centurion, beseeching him,

Capernaum was now Jesus' home-base of operations. After the leper, excluded from the congregation by his physical condition, comes the Centurion, excluded by his ethnicity. The similar sounding story in John 4:46-54 logically and realistically relates to a completely separate incident.

The centurion came beseeching, not as Naaman the Syrian came to Elisha, who demanded a cure, but hat in hand as a humble seeker of assistance. Therefore it would appear he saw more in The Christ than Jesus' own countrymen seemed to see. Even the greatest of men must still approach The Christ as humble beggars.

8:6 And saying, Lord, my servant lieth at home sick of the palsy, grievously tormented.

In this instance the word translated "Lord," *Kurie*, should be translated "Sir". This is a better than average master as most others in that day would have sent the no longer profitable servant away. The servant could not have done more for the master than the master did here for the servant.

The palsy is a disease in which the physician's skill commonly fails; it is therefore a great evidence of his faith in the power of The Christ, to come to Him for a cure, which was beyond the power of natural means to effect.

8:7 And Jesus saith unto him, I will come and heal him.

8:8 The centurion answered and said, Lord, I am not worthy that thou shouldest come under my roof: but speak the word only, and my servant shall be healed.

The Centurion knew that it was not proper for a Jewish Rabbi to enter a Gentile house and instead of considering the Jew to be arrogant as some tend to do he spoke from an attitude of humility which acknowledged the superiority of the Jewish God to all else that are called god.

8:9 For I am a man under authority, having soldiers under me: and I say to this *man,* Go, and he goeth; and to another, Come, and he cometh; and to my servant, Do this, and he doeth *it.*

This centurion seems to have heard enough or seen enough to believe that Jesus acted on the authority of the God of Father Abraham, Isaac, and Jacob, and, being a military officer, was accustomed to obeying orders and giving orders in the knowledge that they would be carried out.

8:10 When Jesus heard *it,* he marvelled, and said to them that followed, Verily I say unto you, I have not found so great faith, no, not in Israel.

8:11 And I say unto you, That many shall come from the east and west, and shall sit down with Abraham, and Isaac, and Jacob, in the kingdom of heaven.

Jesus saw that this Roman had more faith than the vast majority of his fellow Jews. He therefore used this incident to warn the Jews that, in spite of their presumption, many of them would be left out of (excluded from) God's kingdom, but Gentiles from lands far and near would, because of their faith, be included. God has His remnant among all sorts of people. No man's calling or station in this world will function as an excuse for unbelief or lack of piety on the great day of the Lord.

> This was spoken to soften the unreasonable prejudices of the Jews, which they entertained against the Gentiles, and to prepare them to receive their brethren of mankind into religious fellowship with themselves, under the Christian dispensation.

> With Abraham, and Isaac, and Jacob - In the closest communion with the most eminent followers of God. But if we desire to inherit the promises, we must be followers of them who through faith and patience enjoy them. Let us therefore imitate Abraham in his faith, Isaac in his obedience unto death, and Jacob in his hope and expectation of good things to come, amidst all the evils of this life, if we desire to reign with them. – Adam Clarke

> 8:12 But the children of the kingdom shall be cast out into outer darkness: there shall be weeping and gnashing of teeth.

By "the children of the kingdom" are intended the Jews, who were God's peculiar people but who were focused on externals and rejecting their Messiah, The Christ as the only way, the truth and the life. The children of the kingdom who shall be cast out are the "Christians" who focus on externals and reject The Christ as the only way, without which no one may come to the Father.

> 8:13 And Jesus said unto the centurion, Go thy way; and as thou hast believed, *so* be it done unto thee. And his servant was healed in the selfsame hour.
>
> 8:14 And when Jesus was come into Peter's house, he saw his wife's mother laid, and sick of a fever.
>
> 8:15 And he touched her hand, and the fever left her: and she arose, and ministered unto them.

Following "Church" they went to Peter's house where Peter's mother-in-law was sick. Possibly Peter's wife told the men as they entered the house, "Sorry, lunch will be a bit late because my mother is sick." Note, that Jesus did not require an audience to exert His power. The type of fever Peter's mother-in-law had usually lingered for a few days and leaves a person weak for a few days more but Jesus merely helped her stand up and effected an immediate and complete cure. Out of gratitude she ministered to them. True ministry to Christ Jesus is doing, first of all, one's daily duties. The "secular work" to which one has been called is at least as holy a work as preaching when it is done to the glory of Christ and in obedience to Him.

> 8:16 When the even was come, they brought unto him many that were possessed with devils: and he cast out the spirits with *his* word, and healed all that were sick:

When the even was come - The Jews kept their

Sabbath from evening to evening, according to the law, Lev_23:32, From evening to evening shall ye celebrate your Sabbath. And the rabbins say, The Sabbath doth not end but when the sun is set. Hence it was that the sick were not brought out to our Lord till after sun-set, because then the Sabbath was ended.

And healed all that were sick - Not a soul did the Lord Jesus ever reject, who came to him soliciting his aid. Need any sinner despair who comes to him, conscious of his spiritual malady, to be healed by his merciful hand? – Adam Clarke

8:17 That it might be fulfilled which was spoken by Esaias the prophet, saying, Himself took our infirmities, and bare *our* sicknesses.

8:18 Now when Jesus saw great multitudes about him, he gave commandment to depart unto the other side.

8:19 And a certain scribe came, and said unto him, Master, I will follow thee whithersoever thou goest.

It is likely that Matthew is telling us that there were a few scribes numbered among the 120 followers who were coming to Jesus for instruction and one of them speaks up and says he is ready to commit himself to being a devoted disciple of Jesus. Jesus cautions him to carefully count the cost because he is not offering a cushy path. Another one of these scribes seems to say, "I'd like to devote myself totally to You, but just not right now because I have some other business that I must take care of first."

8:20 And Jesus saith unto him, The foxes have holes,

and the birds of the air *have* nests; but the Son of man hath not where to lay *his* head.

There was a certain "name it and claim it" type of preacher who routinely on his television program tried to claim that Jesus was complaining in this verse that His disciples had failed on this particular day to properly secure a nice inn for Him to spend the night on that particular occasion. The man is wrong and not a follower of The Christ but of another.

8:21 And another of his disciples said unto him, Lord, suffer me first to go and bury my father.

One of the other Scribes, most likely, so that we see that one of them was too hasty and committing himself with little thought about what he actually might be committing himself to while another was dragging his feet. Therefore we should take notice that undue delaying in doing is as bad on the one hand, as careless hastiness to commitment is on the other.

"Bury my father: probably his father was old, and apparently near death; but it was a maxim among the Jews, that, if a man had any duty to perform to the dead, he was, for that time, free from the observance of any other precept or duty. The children of Adam are always in extremes; some will rush into the ministry of the Gospel without a call, others will delay long after they are called; the middle way is the only safe one: not to move a finger in the work till the call be given, and not to delay a moment after." – Adam Clarke's Commentary

8:22 But Jesus said unto him, Follow me; and let the dead bury their dead.

Let the dead bury their dead - It was usual for the Jews

to consider a man as dead who had departed from the precepts of the law; and, on this ground, every transgressor was reputed a dead man. Our Lord's saying, being in common use, had nothing difficult in it to a Jew. Natural death is the separation of the body and soul; spiritual death, the separation of God and the soul: men who live in sin are dead to God. – Adam Clarke

8:23 And when he was entered into a ship, his disciples followed him.

8:24 And, behold, there arose a great tempest in the sea, insomuch that the ship was covered with the waves: but he was asleep.

If the name-it-and-claim-it/blab-it-and-grab-it crowd is correct in their claims then there should have only been favorable winds and following seas for the disciples because Jesus was physically present with them. In this world we should not be surprised when storms come our way whether they be natural or spiritual in their composition

A well known feature of Lake Galilee is that storms may blow up quite quickly. It has been speculated that this particular storm may have been stirred up above and beyond that which was natural by Satan, the prince of the power of the air, who saw an opportunity to abort the Author and all the preachers of the Gospel and thereby defeat the purposes of God and thus prevent the plan of salvation being manifested to the world. But that "prince" is no match for the Sovereign Lord of creation.

8:25 And his disciples came to *him,* and awoke him,

saying, Lord, save us: we perish.

8:26 And he saith unto them, Why are ye fearful, O ye of little faith? Then he arose, and rebuked the winds and the sea; and there was a great calm.

Many that have true faith are weak in it from time to time. The followers of The Christ are apt to be disquieted with fears in one stormy day that may not have bothered them at all on a different day; to torment themselves further that things are bad with them and the probability that it will get worse and they come to the brink of despair. Then comes the cry from the soul, "Lord do you care? I am doomed without your help." Those aren't the times when we will utter the KJV style of prayers but the earnest plea

The Christ not only comforts by His presence, He also gloriously delivers by His power. The Christ's help may be deferred, like when His friend Lazarus was ill, but it will be timely and complete. As long as we live in a fallen world it is only natural to occasionally be tossed by tempests but there is no need for the saint to be unduly disturbed. One word from The Christ can change the face of nature, one word of His can restore calm and peace to the most troubled and disturbed soul.

8:27 But the men marveled, saying, What manner of man is this, that even the winds and the sea obey him!

In the Old Testament it was a mark of the sovereignty of God himself that the sea obeyed his orders. Job 38:8-11, Psalm 89:8-9. Perhaps Psalm 107:23-32 was in Matthew's mind as he related this incident and the response of amazement on the part of the disciples.

Every part of the creation, except for man, hears and

obeys the Creator's voice. Sinners have an ear for the world, the devil, and the flesh and until that ear is shut they cannot comprehend the voice of God. When a man's ear is shut to the enemies of his soul it is open to his Friend.

> 8:28 And when he was come to the other side into the country of the Gergesenes, there met him two possessed with devils, coming out of the tombs, exceeding fierce, so that no man might pass by that way.

The Gadarene demoniacs. It is not completely clear whether the site of this incident was near the Jordan outflow (Matthew) or on the eastern shore (Mark/Luke). Both sites have a steep bank and both had mainly Gentile populations nearby, as the presence of a large herd of pigs would require. That doesn't mean the owners of the herd were Jewish, as has been speculated by many, but that would be an interesting sort of poetic justice if they were.

Although some seem to think there may be a difficulty in Matthew in noting two who were possessed of demons while Mark and Luke only mention one, there is no difficulty here as Matthew, a Levite, views things through a different lens. Mark and Luke focused on the more notable person while Matthew would more naturally think of the Jewish law that required two witnesses for a testimony like those offered in 8:28; 9:27; 20:30 where, in each case, a confession is made of Jesus as Son of God or Son of David. Matthew's focus is in showing the authority of Jesus over the demonic powers while the personal details of the men fades into the background.

> 8:29 And, behold, they cried out, saying, What have we to do with thee, Jesus, thou Son of God? art thou come

> hither to torment us before the time?
>
> 8:30 And there was a good way off from them an herd of many swine feeding.
>
> 8:31 So the devils besought him, saying, If thou cast us out, suffer us to go away into the herd of swine.

Matthew leaves out much of the dialogue which captured Peter's attention and quickly gets to the main point, the exorcism.

> 8:32 And he said unto them, Go. And when they were come out, they went into the herd of swine: and, behold, the whole herd of swine ran violently down a steep place into the sea, and perished in the waters.

The panicked stampede provides visible proof of the exorcism to the bystanders. No attention is given to the economic morality, nor the humaneness of the destruction of the herd because with God, unlike with vegans and other like-minded self-centered pagans, the liberation of two men takes precedence over such considerations.

> 8:33 And they that kept them fled, and went their ways into the city, and told every thing, and what was befallen to the possessed of the devils.

The local reaction is thoroughly understandable; Jesus is not always a comfortable person to have around. It is not unlike driving along and suddenly seeing a police car; you quickly check your speed and run through a mental checklist to ensure you are observing all the rules of the road.

"All down through the ages the world has been refusing Jesus because it prefers its pigs," P.P. Levertoff, St Matthew (1940), pg 26

Matthew makes no mention of the men's mission to their own people because his interest and focus in the mission to Gentiles is, for him, a post Gospel writing development and the primary purpose of this gospel account is to show the Jewish people that their Messiah is this Jesus who has authority over all creation and supernatural powers. If Jesus has cured you show it by causing joy where you have caused much misery.

> 8:34 And, behold, the whole city came out to meet Jesus: and when they saw him, they besought *him* that he would depart out of their coasts.

Perhaps it would be better to understand "They of the village" or "they of this suburb" whose economic livelihood was entwined with the care and marketing of the herd came out to deal with this exorcist. They cared much more about their hogs than human souls the devils were destroying, as so often happens today. They couldn't comprehend the benefit of having The Christ in their city.

Even today Jesus is often deemed dangerous rather than delightful to have around. Folks tend to like The Christ as the physician of their body, but not of their soul. Their "Depart from us" is the foreboding of His "Depart from Me." (Matt 25:41) Those who refuse and continue to refuse to let Him be their Lord will find Him refusing to be their Savior at the last day. See Luke 19:27

CHAPTER NINE

9:1 And he entered into a ship, and passed over, and came into his own city.

Capernaum and, no doubt, at Peter's house which He is believed to have made the base of His operations when in that vicinity.

9:2 And, behold, they brought to him a man sick of the palsy, lying on a bed: and Jesus seeing their faith said unto the sick of the palsy; Son, be of good cheer; thy sins be forgiven thee.

Matthew omits descriptive details which may or may not indicate whether he was an eyewitness. His focus is the miracle and the dialogue which introduce a new aspect of Jesus' authority. Jesus' declaration "Your sins are forgiven" seems scarcely relevant to this man's condition, but in a culture that linked illness to sin this was not so. Make no mistake, Jesus does not say here or anywhere else that a given illness is the result of sin, but to that patient, this assurance is a great encouragement.

9:3 And, behold, certain of the scribes said within

themselves, This *man* blasphemeth.

These Scribes are not among those following Jesus as part of the greater group of disciples. They actually are doing their job in that they are scrutinizing this Prophet of Galilee to see if what He says and does is acceptable to the orthodoxy. Jesus purposefully antagonized them, He doesn't actually allow anyone to remain neutral towards Him; if He were only a man, as they imagined, then they could have been right because the forgiving of sins is the prerogative of God, not man.

9:4 And Jesus knowing their thoughts said, Wherefore think ye evil in your hearts?

9:5 For whether is easier, to say, *Thy* sins be forgiven thee; or to say, Arise, and walk?

Which is easier to say? Obviously it is easier to say "Your sins are forgiven," because who can prove whether or not it has been done?

9:6 But that ye may know that the Son of man hath power on earth to forgive sins, (then saith he to the sick of the palsy,) Arise, take up thy bed, and go unto thine house.

9:7 And he arose, and departed to his house.

9:8 But when the multitudes saw *it,* they marvelled, and glorified God, which had given such power unto men.

Matthew focuses on the response of the people whereas Peter focused on the response of the delegation from Jerusalem in his Gospel account regarding this incident.

9:9 And as Jesus passed forth from thence, he saw a man, named Matthew, sitting at the receipt of custom: and he saith unto him, Follow me. And he arose, and followed him.

The call of Matthew, the penman of this Gospel account.

The tax office at Capernaum would be concerned with goods crossing the frontier of Antipas' tetrachy either across the lake from Decapolis or across the Jordan from Philip's tetrarchy which would therefore make him a customs official for Herod Antipas rather than a collector of direct taxes. The same Greek word is employed for both types of tax gatherers who were frequently closely associated with "thieves" and "sinners," even "traitors" to the Jewish people. There is no evidence of previous direct contact between Jesus and this Publican called Matthew, but Jesus is likely becoming fairly well known in Capernaum by the time the call to Matthew takes place. It is not clear whether Jesus gave the name "Matthew," which means "Gift of God" to him or, the more likely that it was the name given by his parents, he is of the tribe of Levi. There is no reason to attempt to whitewash the character of Matthew and make him out to be an honest tax collector, a profession that necessarily attracts dishonest persons for the corruption and temptations it holds forth. Matthew himself owns up to what he was before his conversion as does St Paul, thereby acknowledging and magnifying the grace of The Christ in calling him into His inner circle thereby showing salvation is available to absolutely anyone through Jesus The Christ.

9:10 And it came to pass, as Jesus sat at meat in the house, behold, many publicans and sinners came and sat down with him and his disciples.

Luke specifies that this meal took place at Levi's house. The main focus is that Jesus was willing to sit at a table with "sinners," a term which was also often applied to the common Jewish people who could not or would not keep the scribal rules of tithing and purity, although most often applied to the immoral, heretics, Gentiles, and tax collectors. Jesus' willingness to associate with the undesirables is a prominent feature of the Gospel portrait.

9:11 And when the Pharisees saw *it,* they said unto his disciples, Why eateth your Master with publicans and sinners?

The reaction is inevitable. The Pharisees prided themselves in the outward performance of the law.

9:12 But when Jesus heard *that,* he said unto them, They that be whole need not a physician, but they that are sick.

The difference between Jesus and the Pharisees lies partly in their perception of priorities in the purposes of God: for the Pharisees the first priority is performance of regulations, for Jesus it is people and a healer must sometimes get his hands dirty.

9:13 But go ye and learn what *that* meaneth, I will have mercy, and not sacrifice: for I am not come to call the righteous, but sinners to repentance.

The quotation of Hosea 6:6 is introduced by a Rabbinic formula, "Go and learn what this means," which means reflect on the deeper meaning rather than on the shallow surface appearance of the text. Hosea had objected to a religion that was all external. They seemed incapable of comprehending that they were guilty of performing merely superficial religion which God has repeatedly made clear that He Himself rejects. Jesus was saying, those s*inners* who "hunger and thirst after righteousness" were much closer to true righteousness than they were.

9:14 Then came to him the disciples of John, saying, Why do we and the Pharisees fast oft, but thy disciples fast not?

9:15 And Jesus said unto them, Can the children of the bridechamber mourn, as long as the bridegroom is with them? but the days will come, when the bridegroom shall be taken from them, and then shall they fast.

Christ referred them to John's testimony of Him, John 3:29.

9:16 No man putteth a piece of new cloth unto an old garment, for that which is put in to fill it up taketh from the garment, and the rent is made worse.

9:17 Neither do men put new wine into old bottles: else the bottles break, and the wine runneth out, and the bottles perish: but they put new wine into new bottles, and both are preserved.

9:18 While he spake these things unto them, behold, there came a certain ruler, and worshipped him, saying, My daughter is even now dead: but come and lay thy hand upon her, and she shall live.

This passage (18-26) is one of Matthew's most notable abbreviations: Mark used 23 verses to relate what Matthew relates in 9.

We have in here an account of a Church leader whose faith contrasts strongly against the obstinate unbelief of many of his contemporaries. While faith is not mentioned explicitly in this account, the ruler's confidence in Jesus' healing power is closely parallel to the Centurion's in Matthew 8:8-9.

9:19 And Jesus arose, and followed him, and *so did* his

disciples.

9:20 And, behold, a woman, which was diseased with an issue of blood twelve years, came behind *him,* and touched the hem of his garment:

This woman's disorder rendered her and anything she touched, ceremonially unclean and she was definitely in a desperate situation. She may have had more of a "magical" concept of His healing power in her thinking that if she could just touch the "tassel" of His garment she would be healed but there is no rebuke. Matthew presents the healing as the direct result of Jesus' Word rather than of the tassel touch so that any impression of a "magical" element in the cure is thereby removed. The key is faith of the practical kind as the Centurion in 8:8-9 and elsewhere, but not "faith in faith" as some misconstrue the Savior to be advocating.

9:21 For she said within herself, If I may but touch his garment, I shall be whole.

9:22 But Jesus turned him about, and when he saw her, he said, Daughter, be of good comfort; thy faith hath made thee whole. And the woman was made whole from that hour.

"Thy faith hath made thee whole" seems to be a favorite pronouncement by Jesus. Perhaps it would be better for us if the translators had rendered it, "Thy faith in Me hath made thee whole," so that we would have less of a tendency to be led astray by the Marcionites, also known as, the faith-in-faith advocates. The ancient heresy is back.

The hem of His garment – the tsitsith, or fringes which the Jews were commanded to wear on their garments, Numbers 15:38; Deut 22:12. Jesus was faithful to the Old Testament Law and His objection, found in Matthew 23:5, is to the misuse of the fringe for ostentatious purposes.

9:23 And when Jesus came into the ruler's house, and saw the minstrels and the people making a noise,

> Professional mourners were hired by even the poorest of families. The Mishnah Ketuboth 4:4 specifies that there were to be "Not less than two flutes and one wailing woman."

9:24 He said unto them, Give place: for the maid is not dead, but sleepeth. And they laughed him to scorn.

The maid is not dead, but sleepeth - That is, she is not dead so as to continue under the power of death; but shall be raised from it as a person is from natural sleep.

> **They laughed him to scorn** - Καεγελωουν, they ridiculed him; from κα, intensive, and γελαω, I laugh: - they grinned a ghastly smile, expressive of the contempt they felt for his person and knowledge. People of the world generally ridicule those truths which they neither comprehend nor love, and deride those who publish them; but a faithful minister of God, (copying the example of Christ), keeps on his way, and does the work of his Lord and Master. – Adam Clarke Commentary

9:25 But when the people were put forth, he went in, and took her by the hand, and the maid arose.

Jesus kicked the professional mourners out.

> **He - took her by the hand, and the maid arose** - The fountain of life thus communicating its vital energy to the dead body. Where death has already taken place, no power but that of the great God can restore to life; in

such a case, vain is the help of man. So the soul that is dead in trespasses and sins - that is, sentenced to death because of transgression - and is thus dead in law, can only be restored to spiritual life by the mighty power of the Lord Jesus; because He alone has made the atonement, and He alone can pardon transgression. If the spiritually dead person be utterly unconcerned about the state and fate of his soul, let a converted relative either bring him to Christ by leading him to hear the unadulterated Gospel of the kingdom; or bring Christ to him by fervent, faithful, and persevering prayer. — Adam Clarke Commentary

9:26 And the fame hereof went abroad into all that land.

9:27 And when Jesus departed thence, two blind men followed him, crying, and saying, *Thou* Son of David, have mercy on us.

Matthew has two very similar accounts of the healing of two blind men. The one in Matthew 20:29-34 is the same as the account of Bartimaeus in Mark 10:46-52. This one is not related in the other Gospels. The healing of a blind man in Mark 8:22-26 is not related to us by Matthew. During the course of His three and a half year ministry there were, no doubt, many other blind folk who were healed without being documented in the Gospel accounts. These are mentioned so that we may know who Jesus is. They used His Messianic title, "Son of David."

9:28 And when he was come into the house, the blind men came to him: and Jesus saith unto them, Believe ye that I am able to do this? They said unto him, Yea, Lord.

9:29 Then touched he their eyes, saying, According to your

faith be it unto you.

9:30 And their eyes were opened; and Jesus straitly charged them, saying, See *that* no man know *it.*

9:31 But they, when they were departed, spread abroad his fame in all that country.

They just couldn't keep their mouths shut. How sad that many who name the name of Christ today, who have been commanded to tell others and to make disciples, keep their mouths shut. Do they not believe in Him? The silent ones are demonstrating by their silence that they are disbelievers or ashamed of Him.

9:32 As they went out, behold, they brought to him a dumb man possessed with a devil.

9:33 And when the devil was cast out, the dumb spake: and the multitudes marvelled, saying, It was never so seen in Israel.

9:34 But the Pharisees said, He casteth out devils through the prince of the devils.

The Pharisees who made that statement blasphemed and they may have known they were guilty. It is a theory which would be rather ridiculous if it were not the outburst of darkest malignity. Because they saw their power and prestige possibly slipping through their fingers due to the crowds marveling and likely on the verge of accepting Jesus as the long-awaited Messiah the corrupted, self-centered teachers are seeking to downplay and diminish The Christ instead of embracing Him. They are unable to deny the reality of the miracles so they are attempting to discredit them. This time Jesus, apparently, does not respond but later on they will renew this charge and at that time Jesus will refute it with biting sarcasm befitting this vile blasphemy.

Not all the Pharisees were guilty; Nicodemus came to Jesus and essentially declared that he and some others knew Jesus had been sent by God and they recognized the closely scrutinized miracles were proof of that fact.

9:35 And Jesus went about all the cities and villages, teaching in their synagogues, and preaching the gospel of the kingdom, and healing every sickness and every disease among the people.

This is the third Galilean circuit. Jesus visited not only the great cities but the little villages as well because all souls are precious to Him.

9:36 But when he saw the multitudes, he was moved with compassion on them, because they fainted, and were scattered abroad, as sheep having no shepherd.

Jesus was greatly distressed because the people were in a very sorry spiritual condition having been abused by the very ones who were supposed to be their caretakers. They were despised and rejected by the proud Pharisees as not worthy of their time and concern. Centuries later a reformation would have to take place because the old problems had resurfaced. Today many people seem to be willing to seek out the self-serving "shepherds" because The Christ makes them uncomfortable. The ordinary people were "lost sheep" waiting for their Messianic Shepherd while today we have many seeking "shepherds" who will help them feel comfortable in their sins.

9:37 Then saith he unto his disciples, The harvest truly *is* plenteous, but the labourers *are* few;

We find harvest used in the Old Testament as a picture of the coming judgment (Isaiah 27:12; Hosea 6:11; Joel 3:13); John the baptizer speaks along the same line and so does Jesus at another time but here it is the gathering in of those who are ready and looking for The Christ.

9:38 Pray ye therefore the Lord of the harvest, that he will send forth labourers into his harvest.

CHAPTER TEN

10:1 And when he had called unto *him* his twelve disciples, he gave them power *against* unclean spirits, to cast them out, and to heal all manner of sickness and all manner of disease.

> This is the first place where the word is used. Αποςολος an apostle, comes from αποςελλω, I send a message. The word was anciently used to signify a person commissioned by a king to negotiate any affair between him and any other power or people. Hence αποςολα and κηρυκες, apostles and heralds, are of the same import in Herodotus. See the remarks at the end of chap. 3.

> It is worthy of notice, that those who were Christ's apostles were first his disciples; to intimate, that men must be first taught of God, before they be sent of God. Jesus Christ never made an apostle of any man who was not first his scholar or disciple. – Adam Clarke

10:2 Now the names of the twelve apostles are these; The first, Simon, who is called Peter, and Andrew his brother;

James *the son* of Zebedee, and John his brother;

10:3 Philip, and Bartholomew; Thomas, and Matthew the publican; James *the son* of Alphaeus, and Lebbaeus, whose surname was Thaddaeus;

10:4 Simon the Canaanite, and Judas Iscariot, who also betrayed him.

10:5 These twelve Jesus sent forth, and commanded them, saying, Go not into the way of the Gentiles, and into *any* city of the Samaritans enter ye not:

This is not a reflection of any anti-Gentile bias but that the Gospel must be first brought to the Jewish people so that they may accept or reject their Messiah whom they were sure was due to be making an appearance. It is true that this gospel reflects the traditional Jewish bias against the Samaritans which Matthew apparently shared based on the fact that this is the only mention he makes of them but the wider mission comes later. Following the resurrection, they were told that they should be witnesses first "In Jerusalem, and in all Judea," then "in Samaria," and lastly, "unto the uttermost part of the earth" (Acts 1:8).

10:6 But go rather to the lost sheep of the house of Israel.

The Jewish people were the ancient fold of God; but the people, the sheep, had wandered from their Shepherd. These under-shepherds were being commissioned to bring them back to the Overseer of their souls.

10:7 And as ye go, preach, saying, The kingdom of heaven is at hand.

Proclaim salvation to all you meet. Wherever the followers of The Christ go they encounter lost, ruined souls;

and wherever they find them they should proclaim Jesus, and His willingness and ability to save. This is so vastly superior to Muhammad's counterfeit system, or any other, which cannot save anyone.

10:8 Heal the sick, cleanse the lepers, raise the dead, cast out devils: freely ye have received, freely give.

"Raise the dead" is lacking in many manuscripts and is not likely to have happened at this time as there is no evidence that any of the disciples did that for any person prior to the resurrection of The Christ.

> **Freely ye have received, freely give** - A rule very necessary, and of great extent. A minister or laborer in the Gospel vineyard, though worthy of his comfortable support while in the work, should never preach for hire, or make a secular traffic of a spiritual work. What a scandal is it for a man to traffic with gifts which he pretends, at least, to have received from the Holy Ghost, of which he is not the master, but the dispenser. He who preaches to get a living, or to make a fortune, is guilty of the most infamous sacrilege. – Adam Clarke

10:9 Provide neither gold, nor silver, nor brass in your purses,

This was not a call to asceticism but an assurance, of sorts, that proper food and lodging would be provided as the Spirit of God moved upon certain individuals.

10:10 Nor scrip for *your* journey, neither two coats, neither shoes, nor yet staves: for the workman is worthy of his meat. They weren't to bring extra shoes or any other provisions one would normally bring along on a journey. This particular mission trip was to be done as though in haste; the sheep are lost, pluck them out of the jaws of the destroyer.

10:11 And into whatsoever city or town ye shall enter, enquire who in it is worthy; and there abide till ye go thence.

They were to look for someone willing and able to accommodate them. While not spelled out at this time, they were not to be an undue burden to their hosts. In the beginning of the Gospel era, all of The Christ's preachers were itinerant.

10:12 And when ye come into an house, salute it.

The salutation is not a mere formality. The blessing, upon being spoken was considered a potent force which goes out and is effective, but not automatic, if the intended recipient possesses a wrong attitude the blessing will return to the issuer. It is better than an uncashed check given back to the issuer because the Spirit of God has added value to it the instant it was spoken.

10:13 And if the house be worthy, let your peace come upon it: but if it be not worthy, let your peace return to you.

10:14 And whosoever shall not receive you, nor hear your words, when ye depart out of that house or city, shake off the dust of your feet.

Jesus knew His message, and His messengers, would meet with rejection as well as acceptance. The result would be a division among men which they were not to gloss over but to emphasize: "Shake off the dust" was a dramatic gesture of repudiation in that culture. Too many namby-pamby people today would scream that you are being too judgmental if they see you do something like that today.

10:15 Verily I say unto you, It shall be more tolerable for the land of Sodom and Gomorrha in the day of judgment, than for that city.

That people and that place which is marked out as in opposition to the message of Jesus has set themselves up to face a judgment more severe even than that of Sodom and Gomorrah, which were the most notorious centers of inequity in the Old Testament. These had the privilege of a clearer call to repentance than they and therefore their guilt is counted as greater. You ACLU and Freedom From Religion Foundation (FRFF) types, as well as anyone of a similar sort of mindset, should be very worried; I know that you are not now, but the day is absolutely guaranteed to come when you will wish you had been.

> **In the day of judgment** - Or, punishment, - κρισεως. Perhaps not meaning the day of general judgment, nor the day of the destruction of the Jewish state by the Romans; but a day in which God should send punishment on that particular city, or on that person, for their crimes. So the day of judgment of Sodom and Gomorrah, was the time in which the Lord destroyed them by fire and brimstone, from the Lord out of heaven.
>
> If men are thus treated for not receiving the preachers of the Gospel, what will it be to despise the Gospel itself, to decry it, to preach the contrary, to hinder the preaching of it, to abuse those who do preach it in its purity, or to render it fruitless by calumnies and lies! Their punishment, our Lord intimates, shall be greater than that inflicted on the inhabitants of Sodom and Gomorrah! – Adam Clarke

10:16 Behold, I send you forth as sheep in the midst of

wolves: be ye therefore wise as serpents, and harmless as doves.

While this verse clearly applies to the first apostolic mission it should not be confused with the concept of pacifism at all costs. Professional pacifism can be a cover for criminal cowardice; that which will annoy the "pacifist" exposes the core of his character and agenda.

Christians in all ages have found that they must live and witness in a hostile world. There are occasional periods and places where some Christians are able to live in relative peace and safety but that often only means the devil and his minions are regrouping and reloading after having suffered a setback in their evil agenda and waiting for a more opportune time.

If wicked men don't oppose the Pastor then the Pastor is doing something wrong. If wicked men don't oppose the people in the pew then the people in the pew are doing something wrong. The saints should embrace us but the sinner should be made aware of his need to get himself right with God.

We also must be wise enough to comprehend when defensive aggression is required to halt the advances of evil. They were not to be like sheep in their attitude but prudent. Christians are not to be gullible or naïve nor are they to be rogues but irreproachably honest.

10:17 But beware of men: for they will deliver you up to the councils, and they will scourge you in their synagogues;

If they hate the Biblical Jesus then it only stands to reason that they would hate the genuine followers of Jesus; those who compromise Christ's commands with the world are not

Christian no matter what they themselves may claim; the Scripture has already judged them.

You may well ask, "Who are the genuine followers of Jesus because we have so many denominations?"

1. Those who reject the Holy Bible, no matter what their excuse, have a problem.
2. Those who reject the Biblical Jesus as the only way of salvation have an even more serious problem.

The Gospel of Jesus according to Luke records how Jesus feels regarding those who want a different way to Heaven than through Him, "Bring those who did not want Me to reign over them and slay them in My presence."

10:18 And ye shall be brought before governors and kings for my sake, for a testimony against them and the Gentiles.

For my sake Does not imply that the charge is explicitly that of following Jesus, but that it resulted from obedience to The Christ.

The mention of "governors and kings" does suggest a bigger picture than just this missionary campaign. After the resurrection they would render testimony both to Jew and Gentile of the truth and power of the Gospel of the holy one of God, Jesus The Christ.

10:19 But when they deliver you up, take no thought how or what ye shall speak: for it shall be given you in that same hour what ye shall speak.

The prospect of trial before governors and kings would naturally terrify the humble disciple. However this is also covered by the "Do not be anxious" of 6:25-34 because God will provide that which is needed. But this does not give us permission to be lazy in our preparatory work and studies.

10:20 For it is not ye that speak, but the Spirit of your Father which speaketh in you.

This was an extraordinary promise, and was literally fulfilled to those first preachers of the Gospel; and to them it was essentially necessary, because the New Testament dispensation was to be fully opened by their extraordinary inspiration. There are some who suggest that the Apostles were ignorant, unlearned men; that, in and of itself, is an ignorant statement, at best, on their part. At worst, it demonstrates the unwillingness to comply with the commands of The Christ and/or evilness in their own heart.

When the Disciples were called to follow The Christ they were enrolled into the most prestigious university that has ever existed for a three and a half year intensive course of study. They failed an exam on the night that their Professor was betrayed into the hands of the willfully ignorant and they had to have a few more days of remedial training but they were far from being ignorant and unlearned by that time. In a certain measure, it may be truly said, that the Holy Spirit animates and empowers the true students of The Christ, and enables them to speak above and beyond whatever their level of training.

10:21 And the brother shall deliver up the brother to death, and the father the child: and the children shall rise up against *their* parents, and cause them to be put to death.

10:22 And ye shall be hated of all *men* for my name's sake: but he that endureth to the end shall be saved.

10:23 But when they persecute you in this city, flee ye into another: for verily I say unto you, Ye shall not have gone over the cities of Israel, till the Son of man be come.

The Christian must not be cowed into giving up his mission nor should he waste his time flogging a dead horse. They are not to imprudently draw upon themselves persecution by being tactless but they may not compromise the teaching of Scripture. Flight is criminal in those mercenary preachers who, through love to their flesh and their property, abandon the flock of The Christ to the wolf.

10:24 The disciple is not above *his* master, nor the servant above his lord.

A person is not a scholar of The Christ unless he learns His doctrine; and he does not learn it as he ought unless he puts it in practice. Wisdom is needed when putting that doctrine into practice so as not to cause offense when it is not appropriate and to cause offense when appropriate.

10:25 It is enough for the disciple that he be as his master, and the servant as his lord. If they have called the master of the house Beelzebub, how much more *shall they call* them of his household?

Will not the world love its own and them only? It is true that it does not even always love its own therefore how much more so will it despise those who belong to the Kingdom of Light.

Beelzebul/Beelzebub appears in a few different forms, one meaning fly god and another dung god with the latter being the one of utmost contempt. Change "dung" to its "S" word meaning and you more clearly see the vulgarity in their epithet against the pure and holy Lamb of God.

10:26 Fear them not therefore: for there is nothing covered, that shall not be revealed; and hid, that shall not be known.

10:27 What I tell you in darkness, *that* speak ye in light: and what ye hear in the ear, *that* preach ye upon the housetops.

He speaks to them about something, a practice, which they were familiar with. His meaning is that everything that He was telling them was for the benefit of all mankind and nothing that He taught them was to be kept back and nothing was. It encompassed the idea of not merely repeating His public discourses but the explanations and the private discourses He had with them. Everything was to be told; there is no secret knowledge kept in reserve only for a select inner circle.

The practice referenced was that the doctor who explained the law in Hebrew had an interpreter close by him into whose ear he whispered what he said; this interpreter then spoke aloud to the people what had been whispered to him.

In the Gospel accounts we consistently see the disciples failing to see and comprehend what The Christ is communicating to them. As we ponder that we seem to see a disappointed look on His face as they fail and get confused. But in the Acts we see them preaching clear, strong, definite truth from Jerusalem to Rome and all points in between.

10:28 And fear not them which kill the body, but are not able to kill the soul: but rather fear him which is able to destroy both soul and body in hell.

"It is prudent to give up the body in order to save the soul; it is like casting the cargo of the vessel into the sea to preserve the crew from destruction," Quesnell.

The emphasis here is on the total and final destruction in hell, as opposed to the limited nature of merely physical death. Destroy (apolesai) means loss or ruin as well as a literal destruction but the expression does not necessarily imply, though it can, annihilation of the finally impenitent as opposed to eternal punishment. Men may terminate the physical existence but they cannot touch the real person. Compared to the fate which awaits the disobedient and them which reject The Christ, martyrdom is a far less fearful prospect.

10:29 Are not two sparrows sold for a farthing? and one of them shall not fall on the ground without your Father. Submit to God in the midst of all trials for comfort and confidence for He is fully aware of your situation, even more so than you are.

10:30 But the very hairs of your head are all numbered.

10:31 Fear ye not therefore, ye are of more value than many sparrows.

Nothing in God's world is outside of His concern however Christians and sparrows do die therefore we should understand that this statement does not promise escape from suffering or death, sometimes we may wish it did, but we have this wonderful assurance, He still has an intimate knowledge of and concern for His children.

10:32 Whosoever therefore shall confess me before men, him will I confess also before my Father which is in heaven.

10:33 But whosoever shall deny me before men, him will I also deny before my Father which is in heaven.

The human heart is, due its fallen nature, decidedly hostile to the intent and spirit of the gospel.

"I will keep my religion to myself," says one; if you will not confess The Christ to men then He will renounce you before, in the presence of, God.

Let it always be remembered, that to be renounced by The Christ is to have Him neither for a savior nor for a mediator. Thus there is a fate worse than human persecution; to be repudiated, or renounced, by Jesus Himself before the Father. The "first hearers" of this statement heard, in this statement, a clear declaration from Jesus that He, not God the Father, it the final determiner as to whom will be allowed to enter into and abide in Heaven and who will not. Rejection by humans is temporary; rejection by Jesus is forever.

Fear of men is a self-interested, self-deluding cowardice; fear of God is a healthy response of awe and obedience. The latter is positively commended upon throughout the Bible while the former is condemned by God as well as by men everywhere.

10:34 Think not that I am come to send peace on earth: I came not to send peace, but a sword.

The peace Messiah brings is much more than the absence of armed conflict which is all many short-sighted and small minded men tend to think of and to claim to hope for. The peace Messiah Jesus brings is a restored relationship with the God of Father Abraham, Isaac, and Jacob. The sword Messiah Jesus brings is a sharp social division which severs even the closest family ties when one individual chooses a personal response of following Messiah and another chooses to reject the lordship of Messiah Jesus and pursue another path. The division is inevitable, even in this world, between those who embrace Jesus and those who reject The Christ. The rejecter may feel rejected by the rejectee without realizing the rejectee is offering reconciliation rather than retribution as He tries to warn that the day will come at the last when the finally impenitent one will suffer, without remedy, the consequences of his own bad choices.

The followers of Jesus must not expect ease and comfort. The PMA people want their followers to believe that followers of The Christ will not suffer setbacks or persecution but Jesus Himself warned otherwise. The majority of the Jewish religious leadership in Jesus' day were proclaiming practically the same message as the prosperity gospel preachers of our own day. Therefore Solomon's words still ring true, "Nothing new under the sun," and the "God has to bless you" preachers are practicing the same old heresies from many centuries ago. The followers of The Christ must constantly and consistently put loyalty to Jesus before all other loyalties, and this may result in conflict and division, even within our own families. They who strive to be obedient to Jesus must be prepared for hardship, persecution and possibly death but in the end, win or lose in this life, they shall be the ultimate winners. In sacrificing the life of self-pleasing in order to please their Lord, they will find life in its truest sense (34-39).

All who welcome Jesus' messengers into their homes are really welcoming Jesus who sent them, and God the Father who sent Him. Help given to Jesus' messengers will be rewarded as if given to Jesus Himself.

10:35 For I am come to set a man at variance against his father, and the daughter against her mother, and the daughter in law against her mother in law.

Jesus does not come to poison family relationships but the division comes about due to one embracing Him and another rejecting Him. The spirit of the Messiah can have no union with the spirit of the world so that even a father, while in an unconverted state will oppose his godly child. Therefore the spirit that is in those who sin against God is opposed to that spirit which is in the followers of the holy one of God. It is therefore the spirits then that are in opposition, and not the persons, per se.

> The unrest of a Christless soul, a Christless nation, a Christless world, is really the beginning of a vital process, which in its first stages is always a travail. The Lord is not afraid of the storm of strife and frenzy which He stirs in the world. We think these are death pains; He knows that they are birth pains through which the glorious golden future is being born. – J. B. Brown, B.A.

10:36 And a man's foes *shall be* they of his own household.

Jesus is actually referring them to their own traditions that were being taught in that day. They held that in the time just before the arrival of the age of the Messiah this would be the case. This began to take place in earnest not long after their rejection of the Messiah. The historian Josephus recorded the desolation of that time. Therefore through the just judgment of God, those who rejected the Messiah and the salvation He offered found themselves to be partakers of the devil's condemnation.

Although they preached good news and did good works, the apostles could expect persecution even from those who had formerly been near and dear to them because of choices made regarding the person of The Christ. Although they would meet opposition from friends and relatives they were to press on diligently and earnestly in their mission in the assurance they were pursuing the correct path which leads to eternal life.

10:37 He that loveth father or mother more than me is not worthy of me: and he that loveth son or daughter more than me is not worthy of me.

He whom we love the most is he whom we strive most to please, and whose will and interests we prefer in most, if not all, cases. True discipleship may bring a conflict of loyalties, and in that case, following Jesus must take precedence over the natural love of family which must take second place to loyalty to The Christ. Matthew's version correctly relates the Semitic idiom which is that the love towards Jesus must be greater than the love towards even the dearest family member. Dr Luke's gospel account doesn't relate this idiom to us quite as well.

The Christ deserves our supreme love; no mere human being has sacrificed so much for us as He.

10:38 And he that taketh not his cross, and followeth after me, is not worthy of me.

So that our Lord was saying that the one who was unwilling to risk everything, including loss of his own physical life, for the cause of The Christ cannot be counted as a disciple.

Jesus bore a far heavier cross than mine and He will give me the grace to carry it. "Welcome the cross of Christ, and bear it triumphantly; but see that it be indeed Christ's cross, and not thine own." - Wilcox

10:39 He that findeth his life shall lose it: and he that loseth his life for my sake shall find it.

"He that would lose nothing, must learn to have nothing." – Farindon

The pithiness of this paradoxical maxim revolves around the double sense attached to the word "life" – the lower and the higher; the physical and the spiritual; the temporal and the eternal. Whatever a man sacrifices to The Christ is never lost, for he finds it again in God.

10:40 He that receiveth you receiveth me, and he that receiveth me receiveth him that sent me.

The kindness shown to the disciple of The Christ Jesus counts as though shown directly unto Himself. We must constantly carefully consider that we are to always to be the ambassador of The Christ as He was the ambassador of God. Therefore our Lord asserts that the authority of the faithful disciple "is Mine, as Mine is My Father's."

10:41 He that receiveth a prophet in the name of a prophet shall receive a prophet's reward; and he that receiveth a righteous man in the name of a righteous man shall receive a righteous man's reward.

He that receiveth a prophet - a teacher, not a foreteller of future events, for this is not always the meaning of the word; but one commissioned by God to teach the doctrines of eternal life. It is no small honor to receive into one's house a minister of Jesus Christ. Every person is not admitted to exercise the sacred ministry; but none are excluded from partaking of its grace, its spirit, and its reward. If the teacher should be weak, or even if he should be found afterwards to have been worthless, yet the person who has received him in the name, under the sacred character, of an evangelist, shall not lose his reward; because what he did he did for the sake of Christ, and through love for his Church. Many sayings of this kind are found among the rabbins, and this one is common: "He who receives a learned man, or an elder, into his house, is the same as if he had received the Shekinah." And again: "He who speaks against a faithful pastor, it is the same as if he had spoken against God himself." See Schoettgen. – Adam Clarke

10:42 And whosoever shall give to drink unto one of these little ones a cup of cold *water* only in the name of a disciple, verily I say unto you, he shall in no wise lose his reward.

Water was and is an essential act of courtesy in that arid land. It is taken for granted and deserves no reward however even that very simple and expected act will be rewarded by God. However, if a far better gift could and should have been given God is fully aware of that fact as well and will take note. The gift and the motive come under Divine notice of the "God who sees."

But a cup of water in the eastern countries was not a matter of small worth. In India, the Hindoos go sometimes a great way to fetch it, and then boil it that it may do the less hurt to travelers when they are hot; and, after that, they stand from morning to night in some great road, where there is neither pit nor rivulet, and offer it, in honor of their god, to be drunk by all passengers. This necessary work of charity, in these hot countries, seems to have been practised by the more pious and humane Jews; and our Lord assures them that, if they do this in his name, they shall not lose their reward. See the Asiatic Miscellany, vol. ii. p. 142. – Adam Clarke

The history of nations and individuals proves how the past acts upon the future. Things done out of The Christ, having no connection with His love, will perish. The promise of our Lord shows how every simple act done with reference to Him is made to react upon ourselves in a way we should not anticipate apart from revelation.

CHAPTER ELEVEN

11:1 And it came to pass, when Jesus had made an end of commanding his twelve disciples, he departed thence to teach and to preach in their cities.

During this first mission Jesus sent His disciples upon they apparently encountered little opposition, based on the reports they gave following that mission. Jesus prepared them for what they could expect in the future, though. The 12 were actually expecting nothing but pomp and power to proceed their way but Jesus was already trying to warn against the blab-it-and-grab-it prosperity gospel practitioners and help them to have a correct understanding of what they could realistically expect from the world.

Because they were properly warned what to expect they were able to bear up following Pentecost under things which could have been a serious shock to their faith but instead it became a confirmation for them that they were proceeding down the correct path.

Wicked men are like wolves whose nature it is to destroy and devour the sheep. God's people and His ministers are like sheep among them and commonly easy prey to them.

That we are as sheep among wolves is frightful but it is The Christ that sends us forth and that is greatly comforting for we know that He will protect and bear us safely home.

Those whom The Christ loves the world tends to dislike. The world tries to remake The Christ into its own image but those who bear the image of The Christ stand as stark reminders of a reality that cannot be changed.

The followers of The Christ must expect to be apprehended and arraigned as malefactors. Every day of peace and security is a cause of praise, not only to God, but to those who have had to endure hardship before us to help bring about the time of peace. The restless malice is resistless malice and the malefactors frequently succeed in delivering the Christ followers up to their councils.

A deal of mischief is often done to good men under the cloak of law and justice. In the place of judgment there is often wickedness, persecuting wickedness, Eccl 3:16. Christians can expect in this world to encounter trouble, not only from morally inferior magistrates in the councils, but from governors and kings, the "supreme" magistrates of this world. To be brought unto them, under such bleak representations as were commonly made of Christ's followers, was dreadful and dangerous.

They, the disciples, must not be surprised to be even put to death for His sake. The malice of the enemies of God rages so high as to inflict this; it is the blood of the saints that they thirst after. The wisdom of The Christ sometimes permits this, knowing how to make the blood of His martyrs the seal of the truth, and the seed of the Church. By this noble army's not loving their lives to the death, Satan has been vanquished, and the kingdom of The Christ and its interests greatly advanced to the honor of God and His truth.

> 11:2 Now when John had heard in the prison the works of Christ, he sent two of his disciples,

John's arrest was mentioned in 4:12; the full story of his imprisonment will wait until 14:3. John had been certain that Jesus was The Christ, but now, in the dungeon, he was no longer so sure. Jesus' ministry was not matching up with popular theology.

Notice that Jesus does not tell John's disciples to go back and tell John "Suck it up, buttercup." That is, in a sense, what John and the Pharisees were actually expecting from The Messiah; that is because they were wanting and expecting the arrival of the conquering Messiah. However the message and ministry for that day was the suffering servant who brings salvation has arrived. Today the message is more appropriately along the line of "Suck it up, buttercup, you're in the army of the King of Kings who is about to bring justice and judgment upon the world for its rebellion." Therefore, Christian, put on your full armor and be prepared.

> 11:3 And said unto him, Art thou he that should come, or do we look for another?

It would seem that, of all people, John would've been the least likely to have had doubts and, therefore, some have tried to suggest that is was really John's friends who actually had the doubts. Rather than try to suggest such a thing, it is more profitable to us to recognize and consider the fact that even the strongest of saints may wobble in a weak moment in their walk and be desperately in need of a faith lift. That is what Jesus does for John, his friends, and all who follow Jesus, The Christ. He did not merely say something to the effect of "Of course, I'm the one you were looking for," He proves it by action. Words would likely have made John feel bad for entertaining doubt but the actions were a more powerful and positive affirmation of the truth that Jesus is the holy one of God and the way of salvation.

> 11:4 Jesus answered and said unto them, Go and shew John again those things which ye do hear and see:

Go and show John the things - ye do hear and see - Christ would have men to judge of him and of others by their works. This is the only safe way of judging. A man is not to be credited because he professes to know such and such things; but because he demonstrates by his conduct that his pretensions are not vain. – Adam Clarke

If the fruit is good we may judge the tree to be good.

> 11:5 The blind receive their sight, and the lame walk, the lepers are cleansed, and the deaf hear, the dead are raised up, and the poor have the gospel preached to them.

It was foretold that Messiah would work miraculous cures. Isaiah 30:4-6

It was foretold that Messiah would preach to the poor Isaiah 61:1

It was foretold that the world would be offended by the Messiah Isaiah 8:14

The disciples of John and John himself were thrilled and encouraged by what Jesus did however The Christ's opponents were annoyed. Therefore what was the sweet savor of life to one was the aroma of death to the other.

The poor have the Gospel preached to them - And what was this Gospel? Why, the glad tidings that Jesus Christ came into the world to save sinners: that he opens the eyes of the blind; enables the lame to walk with an even, steady, and constant pace in the way of holiness; cleanses the lepers from all the defilement of their sins; opens the ears of the deaf to hear his pardoning words; and raises those who were dead in trespasses and sins to live in union with himself to all eternity. – Adam Clarke

11:6 And blessed is *he,* whosoever shall not be offended in me.

Take offence – be tripped up by. Many were tripped up by Jesus when His style of ministry and message failed to tally with their expectations even though He showed them how the Scripture pointed them to Him and it.

11:7 And as they departed, Jesus began to say unto the multitudes concerning John, What went ye out into the wilderness to see? A reed shaken with the wind?

As John's disciples start to leave Jesus begins to deliver a glowing tribute to John. John was not a weak messenger easily swayed by the pressure of human opinion. John stood up to those in power and challenged them rather than let himself be intimidated. In this tribute to His friend, Jesus concludes with an indictment of His opponents.

A reed shaken with the wind? - An emblem of an irresolute, unsteady mind, which believes and speaks one thing to-day, and another to-morrow. Christ asks these Jews if they had ever found anything in John like this: Was he not ever steady and uniform in the testimony he bore to me? The first excellency which Christ notices in John was his steadiness; convinced once of the truth, he continued to believe and assert it. This is essentially necessary to every preacher, and to every private Christian. He who changes about from opinion to opinion, and from one sect or party to another, is never to be depended on; there is much reason to believe that such a person is either mentally weak, or has never been rationally and divinely convinced of the truth. – Adam Clarke

11:8 But what went ye out for to see? A man clothed in soft raiment? behold, they that wear soft *clothing* are in kings' houses.

11:9 But what went ye out for to see? A prophet? yea, I say unto you, and more than a prophet.

John was no self-indulgent, self-interested self-serving tool of the civil powers. Oh no, he was a true prophet, worthy to stand in that noble group of truth-speaking men who carried God's word to a rebellious nation.

John was the capstone of the prophets because he had the privilege and responsibility of announcing the actual arrival of The Messiah. Yet, he belonged to the old order with its inferior blessings, not to the dawning reign of The Christ with its greater blessings and responsibilities. But, make no mistake, the comparison of *greater* and *least* are not comparisons of moral worth but of covenant privilege.

11:10 For this is *he,* of whom it is written, Behold, I send my messenger before thy face, which shall prepare thy way before thee.

John was the instrument in God's hands preparing the people's hearts to receive The Christ. It was due to his faithfulness and preaching that so many hundreds, even thousands, readily attached themselves to The Christ at His appearing as a public teacher.

11:11 Verily I say unto you, Among them that are born of women there hath not risen a greater than John the Baptist: notwithstanding he that is least in the kingdom of heaven is greater than he.

The Rabbis had a saying: "Even the servant maid that passed through the sea with Moses, saw what neither Ezekiel, nor any other of the prophets had seen." The prophets pointed out a Christ that was coming. John pointed out The Christ who was then walking among them. The preachers of the Gospel point out that The Christ suffered, and entered into His glory and repentance and remission from sins are provided through Jesus The Christ.

11:12 And from the days of John the Baptist until now the kingdom of heaven suffereth violence, and the violent take it by force.

These difficult words of Jesus [seem to] mean that the preaching of John "had led to a violent and impetuous thronging to gather round Jesus and his disciples" (Hort, *Judaistic Christianity*, p. 26). – Robertson's Word Pictures

Fighting a way into the kingdom

The Interpreter took the pilgrim again by the hand, and led him into a pleasant place, where was built a stately palace, beautiful to behold; at the sight of which Christian was greatly delighted. He saw also upon the top thereof certain persons walking, who were clothed all in gold. Then said Christian, "May we go in thither?" Then the Interpreter took him, and led him up toward the door of the palace; and behold, at the door stood a great company of men, as desirous to go in, but durst not. There also sat a man at a little distance from the door, at a table-side, with a book and his ink-horn before him, to take the name of him that should enter therein; he saw also that in the doorway stood many men in armour to keep it, being resolved to do to the men that would enter what hurt and mischief they could. Now was Christian somewhat in amaze. At last, when every man started back for fear of the armed men, Christian saw a man of a very stout countenance, come up to the man that sat there to write, saying, "Set down my name, sir; " the which when he had done, he saw the man draw his sword, and put a helmet upon his head, and rush toward the door upon the armed men, who laid upon him with deadly force; but the man, not at all discouraged, fell to cutting and hacking most fiercely. So that, after he had received and given many wounds to those that attempted to keep him out, he cut his way through them all, and pressed forward into the palace; at which there was a pleasant voice heard from those that were within, even of those that walked upon the top of the palace, saying,

"Come in, Come in,
Eternal glory thou shalt win."

So he went in, and was clothed with such garments as they. (*John Bunyan.*)

The tax-gatherers and heathens, whom the scribes and Pharisees think have no right to the kingdom of the Messiah, filled with holy zeal and earnestness, seize at once on the proffered mercy of the Gospel, and so take the kingdom as if by force from those learned doctors who claimed for themselves the chiefest places in that kingdom. Christ himself said, The tax-gatherers and harlots go before you into the kingdom of God. See the parallel place, Luk 7:28-30. He that will take, get possession of the kingdom of righteousness, peace, and spiritual joy, must be in earnest: all hell will oppose him in every step he takes; and if a man be not absolutely determined to give up his sins and evil companions, and have his soul saved at all hazards, and at every expense, he will surely perish everlastingly. This requires ... earnestness. – Adam Clarke

11:13 For all the prophets and the law prophesied until John.

11:14 And if ye will receive *it*, this is Elias, which was for to come.

This should always be written Elijah, that as strict a conformity as possible might be kept up between the names in the Old Testament and the New. The Prophet Malachi, who predicted the coming of the Baptist in the spirit and power of Elijah, gave the three following distinct characteristics of him. First, That he should be the forerunner and messenger of the Messiah: Behold I send my messenger before me, Mal 3:1. Secondly, That he should appear before the destruction of the second temple: Even the Lord whom ye seek shall suddenly come to his temple, ibid. Thirdly, That he should preach repentance to the Jews; and that, sometime after, the great and terrible day of the Lord should come, and the Jewish land be smitten with a curse, Mal_4:5, Mal_4:6. Now these three characters agree perfectly with the conduct of the Baptist, and what shortly followed his preaching, and have not been found in any one else; which is a convincing proof that Jesus was the promised Messiah. – Adam Clarke

11:15 He that hath ears to hear, let him hear.

Many, if not most, people are ignorant because they choose not to learn.

11:16 But whereunto shall I liken this generation? It is like unto children sitting in the markets, and calling unto their fellows,

11:17 And saying, We have piped unto you, and ye have not danced; we have mourned unto you, and ye have not lamented.

11:18 For John came neither eating nor drinking, and they say, He hath a devil.

A sinner refuses to be persuaded that what he has no desire to imitate can come from God. Therefore John was too austere and aloof. John's humble separation stood in stark contrast to the proud pharisaical separation and thereby annoyed them. Then they complained Jesus was too sociable and should have been more like John. Both were, from their innermost being, holy men of God.

11:19 The Son of man came eating and drinking, and they say, Behold a man gluttonous, and a winebibber, a friend of publicans and sinners. But wisdom is justified of her children.

Outward austerities and observations tend to exalt the man performing them and can easily mask the real character of the person. Jesus chose to set a better example with a strict, but sociable and charitable life and the spending time in doing good thereby setting an example better suited to truly glorifying God and Growing God's kingdom in the here and now.

11:20 Then began he to upbraid the cities wherein most of his mighty works were done, because they repented not:

The more God has done to draw men unto himself, the less excusable are they if they continue in iniquity. If our blessed Lord had not done every thing that was necessary for the salvation of these people, he could not have reproached them for their impenitence. – Adam Clarke

11:21 Woe unto thee, Chorazin! woe unto thee, Bethsaida! for if the mighty works, which were done in you, had been done in Tyre and Sidon, they would have repented long ago in sackcloth and ashes.

The Galilean towns mentioned were not as immoral as the Gentile cities mentioned were; however, because these Galilean towns had witnessed the ministry of Jesus and rejected Him, they would suffer a more severe judgment than the Gentile towns that had never heard of Him. In our day, those nations and people who have had ready access to the Holy Bible and have failed to act correctly will suffer a far more severe judgment than those who did not. This is the proper response to those who utter, "Well, what about those who've never had the opportunity?" "Unto whom much is given, much is required."

> 11:22 But I say unto you, It shall be more tolerable for Tyre and Sidon at the day of judgment, than for you.

> 11:23 And thou, Capernaum, which art exalted unto heaven, shalt be brought down to hell: for if the mighty works, which have been done in thee, had been done in Sodom, it would have remained until this day.

Capernaum had been highly blessed because in it our Lord had dwelt and He did many of His miraculous works there. The word translated "hell" would have been better translated "destruction" in this passage as this city was reduced to a mere archeological curiosity as a result of its neglect of so great a blessing. Holy and just is our God.

> 11:24 But I say unto you, That it shall be more tolerable for the land of Sodom in the day of judgment, than for thee.

> In Jude 1:7, we are told that these persons are suffering the vengeance of eternal fire. The destruction of Sodom and Gomorrah happened A. M. 2107, which was 1897 years before the incarnation. What a terrible thought is this! It will be more tolerable for certain sinners, who have already been damned nearly four thousand years, than for those who, live and die infidels under the Gospel! There are various degrees of punishments in hell, answerable to various degrees of guilt, and the contempt manifested to, and the abuse made of; the

preaching of the Gospel, will rank semi-infidel Christians in the highest list of transgressors, and purchase them the hottest place in hell! Great God! Save the reader from this destruction!

Day of judgment - May either refer to that particular time in which God visits for iniquity, or to that great day in which he will judge the world by the Lord Jesus Christ. The day of Sodom's judgment was that in which it was destroyed by fire and brimstone from heaven, Genesis 19:24; and the day of judgment to Chorazin, Bethsaida, and Capernaum, was the time in which they were destroyed by the Romans. But there is a day of final judgment, when Hades itself, (sinners in a state of partial punishment in the invisible world) shall be cast into the lake of fire and brimstone, which is the second death. See Rev. 20:14. – Adam Clarke

11:25 At that time Jesus answered and said, I thank thee, O Father, Lord of heaven and earth, because thou hast hid these things from the wise and prudent, and hast revealed them unto babes.

11:26 Even so, Father: for so it seemed good in thy sight.

11:27 All things are delivered unto me of my Father: and no man knoweth the Son, but the Father; neither knoweth any man the Father, save the Son, and *he* to whomsoever the Son will reveal *him.*

None can fully comprehend the nature and attributes of God, but Christ; and none can fully comprehend the nature, incarnation, etc., of Christ, but the Father. The full comprehension and acknowledgment of the

Godhead, and the mystery of the Trinity, belong to God alone. – Adam Clarke

11:28 Come unto me, all *ye* that labour and are heavy laden, and I will give you rest.

    The Jews, heavily laden with the burdensome rites of the Mosaic institution, rendered still more oppressive by the additions made by the scribes and Pharisees, who, our Lord says, (Mat_23:4), bound on heavy burdens; and laboring, by their observance of the law, to make themselves pleasing to God, are here invited to lay down their load, and receive the salvation procured for them by Christ.
    Sinners, wearied in the ways of iniquity, are also invited to come to this Christ, and find speedy relief.
    Penitents, burdened with the guilt of their crimes, may come to this Sacrifice, and find instant pardon.
    Believers, sorely tempted, and oppressed by the remains of the carnal mind, may come to this blood, that cleanseth from all unrighteousness; and, purified from all sin, and powerfully succored in every temptation, they shall find uninterrupted rest in this complete Savior.
    All are invited to come, and all are promised rest. If few find rest from sin and vile affections, it is because few come to Christ to receive it. – Adam Clarke

11:29 Take my yoke upon you, and learn of me; for I am meek and lowly in heart: and ye shall find rest unto your souls.

11:30 For my yoke *is* easy, and my burden is light.

CHAPTER TWELVE

12:1 At that time Jesus went on the sabbath day through the corn; and his disciples were an hungred, and began to pluck the ears of corn, and to eat.

In just a few verses (verse 9) we will find that they were on their way to the Synagogue.

> Were hungry. – The former is a mode of expression totally obsolete. How near does the translation of this verse come to our ancient mother-tongue, the Anglo-Saxon! - The Healer went on rest-day over acres: truly his learning knights hungered, and they began to pluck the ear and eat - We may well wonder at the poverty of Christ and his disciples. He was himself present with them, and yet permitted them to lack bread! A man, therefore, is not forsaken of God because he is in want. It is more honorable to suffer the want of all temporal things in fellowship with Christ and his followers, than to have all things in abundance in connection with the world. – Adam Clarke

12:2 But when the Pharisees saw *it,* they said unto him, Behold, thy disciples do that which is not lawful to do upon the sabbath day.

On any ordinary day of the week what the disciples were doing was freely permitted although actual harvesting was forbidden. The rabbinic tradition (in the Mishnah) had grotesquely twisted the meaning of Exodus 34:21 and therefore made unlawful on the Sabbath according to Rabbinic tradition but not the Mosaic Law. Sadly, the Sabbath by this time had thousands of petty rules and regulations surrounding it and the average person probably looked forward to the first day of the week when the heavy yoke of the Sabbath keeping was over.

The Pharisees had quickly pounced and pointed out the multiple transgressions they believed the disciples had committed. It was obvious they expected Jesus to reprimand His disciples and command them to stop. Instead He spoke to the Pharisees in their own language and chastened them in His own way which may be a wee bit hard for us to see because we are, fortunately, not under their traditions and rules although we must remember that we are not at liberty to do as we please because we are to obey the one who is Lord of the Sabbath which is the Christ Jesus. God made the Sabbath to make our lives better and fuller.

12:3 But he said unto them, Have ye not read what David did, when he was an hungred, and they that were with him;

12:4 How he entered into the house of God, and did eat the shewbread, which was not lawful for him to eat, neither for them which were with him, but only for the priests?

12:5 Or have ye not read in the law, how that on the

sabbath days the priests in the temple profane the sabbath, and are blameless?

12:6 But I say unto you, That in this place is *one* greater than the temple.

12:7 But if ye had known what *this* meaneth, I will have mercy, and not sacrifice, ye would not have condemned the guiltless.

12:8 For the Son of man is Lord even of the sabbath day.

12:9 And when he was departed thence, he went into their synagogue:

   Jesus went to the synagogue. It was the act of a man who refused to seek safety and was determined to confront the dangerous situation head on. He was traveling the road to Calvary for that is the path He had set His feet upon which ran from the manger to the tomb. The first thirty years had been a time of fairly quiet preparation but now the time for men to start choosing sides has arrived. They are going to hear His words and see His works. They are going to embrace Him or reject Him. There will be no fence sitting. Pressure is even going to be put on those who wish to be pew potatoes.

12:10 And, behold, there was a man which had *his* hand withered. And they asked him, saying, Is it lawful to heal on the sabbath days? that they might accuse him.

   It was the Sabbath and all work was forbidden and to heal was work. The Mishnah was quite detailed about this. Medical attention could only be given if a life was in danger. An injury could be kept from getting worse but it must not be made better. If a wall fell on someone, enough of it might be cleared away to see if he were dead or alive; if dead, the body must be left until the next day; if alive, he could be helped to a limited extent.

The spectators were very unkind, both to the patient and the Physician. Jesus challenged these experts in the law with two questions and in the process of doing so He put them in a dilemma. They were bound to admit that it was lawful to do good. They were bound to deny that it was lawful to do evil. Then He asked "Is it lawful to save a life or to kill it?"

They were probably startled; Jesus was supposed to be intimidated by their mere presence but He is instead boldly and astutely challenging them and they know their carefully crafted plan has just failed miserably: their trap has been spun around on them and they are the ones caught. Jesus is in charge, not they, and the people know it. However, in their pride and obstinacy they are not going to concede defeat. He has not been to the proper schools! How dare He upstage them! Elitists haven't changed much over the centuries.

12:11 And he said unto them, What man shall there be among you, that shall have one sheep, and if it fall into a pit on the sabbath day, will he not lay hold on it, and lift *it* out?

12:12 How much then is a man better than a sheep? Wherefore it is lawful to do well on the sabbath days.

12:13 Then saith he to the man, Stretch forth thine hand. And he stretched *it* forth; and it was restored whole, like as the other.

Jesus was taking steps to help this man; they were thinking of ways to destroy Jesus. More often than not, sinners would rather destroy the one who reproves them than forsake their sins. Then with a word, not even a physical touch which would have left them a little bit of room for claiming He did something wrong, the healing takes place.

12:14 Then the Pharisees went out, and held a council against him, how they might destroy him.

In their seething rage, the Pharisees left this place and went to out meet with the Herodians to hatch a plot to kill Jesus. Normally, no Pharisee would have anything to do with a Gentile or any man who did not keep the law; they were unclean but there was now a burning hatred kindled in their hearts which would stop at nothing.

The Herodians were the court entourage of Herod and they were continually coming in contact with the Romans and therefore were themselves considered by the Pharisees to be unclean. These Pharisees had chosen sides and were ready to enter into what for them was an unholy alliance.

For the Pharisee, religion was ritual and the rules and regulations were of utmost importance plus they had no sense of sympathy or compassion for the suffering of the people. For Jesus, religion was service; love in action. Although it could be argued that through the Mosaic Law Jesus had given the rituals that were to be followed; the correct performance of a ritual takes back seat to the cry of human need.

12:15 But when Jesus knew *it,* he withdrew himself from thence: and great multitudes followed him, and he healed them all;

12:16 And charged them that they should not make him known:

12:17 That it might be fulfilled which was spoken by Esaias the prophet, saying,

12:18 Behold my servant, whom I have chosen; my beloved, in whom my soul is well pleased: I will put my spirit upon him, and he shall shew judgment to the Gentiles.

12:19 He shall not strive, nor cry; neither shall any man hear his voice in the streets.

12:20 A bruised reed shall he not break, and smoking flax shall he not quench, till he send forth judgment unto victory.

12:21 And in his name shall the Gentiles trust.

12:22 Then was brought unto him one possessed with a devil, blind, and dumb: and he healed him, insomuch that the blind and dumb both spake and saw.

12:23 And all the people were amazed, and said, Is not this the son of David?

12:24 But when the Pharisees heard *it,* they said, This *fellow* doth not cast out devils, but by Beelzebub the prince of the devils.

12:25 And Jesus knew their thoughts, and said unto them, Every kingdom divided against itself is brought to desolation; and every city or house divided against itself shall not stand:

12:26 And if Satan cast out Satan, he is divided against

himself; how shall then his kingdom stand?

12:27 And if I by Beelzebub cast out devils, by whom do your children cast *them* out? therefore they shall be your judges.

12:28 But if I cast out devils by the Spirit of God, then the kingdom of God is come unto you.

12:29 Or else how can one enter into a strong man's house, and spoil his goods, except he first bind the strong man? and then he will spoil his house.

12:30 He that is not with me is against me; and he that gathereth not with me scattereth abroad.

12:31 Wherefore I say unto you, All manner of sin and blasphemy shall be forgiven unto men: but the blasphemy *against* the *Holy* Ghost shall not be forgiven unto men.

12:32 And whosoever speaketh a word against the Son of man, it shall be forgiven him: but whosoever speaketh against the Holy Ghost, it shall not be forgiven him, neither in this world, neither in the *world* to come.

12:33 Either make the tree good, and his fruit good; or else make the tree corrupt, and his fruit corrupt: for the tree is known by *his* fruit.

12:34 O generation of vipers, how can ye, being evil, speak good things? for out of the abundance of the heart the mouth speaketh.

12:35 A good man out of the good treasure of the heart bringeth forth good things: and an evil man out of the evil treasure bringeth forth evil things.

12:36 But I say unto you, That every idle word that men shall speak, they shall give account thereof in the day of judgment.

12:37 For by thy words thou shalt be justified, and by thy words thou shalt be condemned.

12:38 Then certain of the scribes and of the Pharisees answered, saying, Master, we would see a sign from thee.

12:39 But he answered and said unto them, An evil and adulterous generation seeketh after a sign; and there shall no sign be given to it, but the sign of the prophet Jonas:

12:40 For as Jonas was three days and three nights in the whale's belly; so shall the Son of man be three days and three nights in the heart of the earth.

12:41 The men of Nineveh shall rise in judgment with this generation, and shall condemn it: because they repented at the preaching of Jonas; and, behold, a greater than Jonas *is* here.

The men of Nineveh shell rise in judgment - The voice of God, threatening temporal judgments, caused a whole people to repent, who had neither Moses nor Christ, neither the law nor the prophets; and who perhaps never had but this one preacher among them. What judgment may not we expect, if we continue impenitent, after all that God has bestowed upon us? – Clarke

12:42 The queen of the south shall rise up in the judgment with this generation, and shall condemn it: for she came from the uttermost parts of the earth to hear the wisdom of Solomon; and, behold, a greater than Solomon *is* here.

12:43 When the unclean spirit is gone out of a man, he walketh through dry places, seeking rest, and findeth none.

12:44 Then he saith, I will return into my house from whence I came out; and when he is come, he findeth *it* empty, swept, and garnished.

12:45 Then goeth he, and taketh with himself seven other spirits more wicked than himself, and they enter in and dwell there: and the last *state* of that man is worse than the first. Even so shall it be also unto this wicked generation.

12:46 While he yet talked to the people, behold, *his* mother and his brethren stood without, desiring to speak with him.

12:47 Then one said unto him, Behold, thy mother and thy brethren stand without, desiring to speak with thee.

12:48 But he answered and said unto him that told him, Who is my mother? and who are my brethren?

12:49 And he stretched forth his hand toward his disciples, and said, Behold my mother and my brethren!

12:50 For whosoever shall do the will of my Father which is in heaven, the same is my brother, and sister, and mother.

CHAPTER THIRTEEN

13:1 The same day went Jesus out of the house, and sat by the sea side.

13:2 And great multitudes were gathered together unto him, so that he went into a ship, and sat; and the whole multitude stood on the shore.

13:3 And he spake many things unto them in parables, saying, Behold, a sower went forth to sow;

13:4 And when he sowed, some *seeds* fell by the way side, and the fowls came and devoured them up:

13:5 Some fell upon stony places, where they had not much earth: and forthwith they sprung up, because they had no deepness of earth:

13:6 And when the sun was up, they were scorched; and because they had no root, they withered away.

13:7 And some fell among thorns; and the thorns sprung up, and choked them:

13:8 But other fell into good ground, and brought forth fruit, some an hundredfold, some sixtyfold, some thirtyfold.

13:9 Who hath ears to hear, let him hear.

13:10 And the disciples came, and said unto him, Why speakest thou unto them in parables?

13:11 He answered and said unto them, Because it is given unto you to know the mysteries of the kingdom of heaven, but to them it is not given.

13:12 For whosoever hath, to him shall be given, and he shall have more abundance: but whosoever hath not, from him shall be taken away even that he hath.

13:13 Therefore speak I to them in parables: because they seeing see not; and hearing they hear not, neither do they understand.

13:14 And in them is fulfilled the prophecy of Esaias, which saith, By hearing ye shall hear, and shall not understand; and seeing ye shall see, and shall not perceive:

13:15 For this people's heart is waxed gross, and *their* ears are dull of hearing, and their eyes they have closed; lest at any time they should see with *their* eyes, and hear with *their* ears, and should understand with *their* heart, and should be converted, and I should heal them.

13:16 But blessed *are* your eyes, for they see: and your ears, for they hear.

13:17 For verily I say unto you, That many prophets and righteous *men* have desired to see *those things* which ye see, and have not seen *them;* and to hear *those things* which ye hear, and have not heard *them.*

13:18 Hear ye therefore the parable of the sower.

13:19 When any one heareth the word of the kingdom, and understandeth *it* not, then cometh the wicked *one,* and catcheth away that which was sown in his heart. This is he which received seed by the way side.

13:20 But he that received the seed into stony places, the same is he that heareth the word, and anon with joy receiveth it;

13:21 Yet hath he not root in himself, but dureth for a while: for when tribulation or persecution ariseth because of the word, by and by he is offended.

13:22 He also that received seed among the thorns is he that heareth the word; and the care of this world, and the deceitfulness of riches, choke the word, and he becometh unfruitful.

13:23 But he that received seed into the good ground is he that heareth the word, and understandeth *it;* which also beareth fruit, and bringeth forth, some an hundredfold, some sixty, some thirty.

13:24 Another parable put he forth unto them, saying, The kingdom of heaven is likened unto a man which sowed good seed in his field:

13:25 But while men slept, his enemy came and sowed tares among the wheat, and went his way.

13:26 But when the blade was sprung up, and brought forth fruit, then appeared the tares also.

13:27 So the servants of the householder came and said unto him, Sir, didst not thou sow good seed in thy field? from whence then hath it tares?

13:28 He said unto them, An enemy hath done this. The servants said unto him, Wilt thou then that we go and gather them up?

13:29 But he said, Nay; lest while ye gather up the tares, ye root up also the wheat with them.

13:30 Let both grow together until the harvest: and in the time of harvest I will say to the reapers, Gather ye together first the tares, and bind them in bundles to burn them: but gather the wheat into my barn.

13:31 Another parable put he forth unto them, saying, The kingdom of heaven is like to a grain of mustard seed, which a man took, and sowed in his field:

13:32 Which indeed is the least of all seeds: but when it is grown, it is the greatest among herbs, and becometh a tree, so that the birds of the air come and lodge in the branches thereof.

13:33 Another parable spake he unto them; The kingdom of heaven is like unto leaven, which a woman took, and hid in three measures of meal, till the whole was leavened.

13:34 All these things spake Jesus unto the multitude in parables; and without a parable spake he not unto them:

13:35 That it might be fulfilled which was spoken by the prophet, saying, I will open my mouth in parables; I will utter things which have been kept secret from the foundation of the world.

13:36 Then Jesus sent the multitude away, and went into the house: and his disciples came unto him, saying, Declare unto us the parable of the tares of the field.

13:37 He answered and said unto them, He that soweth the good seed is the Son of man;

13:38 The field is the world; the good seed are the children of the kingdom; but the tares are the children of the wicked *one;*

13:39 The enemy that sowed them is the devil; the harvest is the end of the world; and the reapers are the angels.

13:40 As therefore the tares are gathered and burned in the fire; so shall it be in the end of this world.

13:41 The Son of man shall send forth his angels, and they shall gather out of his kingdom all things that offend, and them which do iniquity;

13:42 And shall cast them into a furnace of fire: there shall be wailing and gnashing of teeth.

13:43 Then shall the righteous shine forth as the sun in the kingdom of their Father. Who hath ears to hear, let him hear.

13:44 Again, the kingdom of heaven is like unto treasure hid in a field; the which when a man hath found, he hideth, and for joy thereof goeth and selleth all that he hath, and buyeth that field.

13:45 Again, the kingdom of heaven is like unto a merchant man, seeking goodly pearls:

13:46 Who, when he had found one pearl of great price, went and sold all that he had, and bought it.

13:47 Again, the kingdom of heaven is like unto a net, that was cast into the sea, and gathered of every kind:

13:48 Which, when it was full, they drew to shore, and sat down, and gathered the good into vessels, but cast the bad away.

13:49 So shall it be at the end of the world: the angels shall come forth, and sever the wicked from among the just,

13:50 And shall cast them into the furnace of fire: there shall be wailing and gnashing of teeth.

13:51 Jesus saith unto them, Have ye understood all these things? They say unto him, Yea, Lord.

13:52 Then said he unto them, Therefore every scribe *which is* instructed unto the kingdom of heaven is like unto a man *that is* an householder, which bringeth forth out of his treasure *things* new and old.

13:53 And it came to pass, *that* when Jesus had finished these parables, he departed thence.

13:54 And when he was come into his own country, he taught them in their synagogue, insomuch that they were astonished, and said, Whence hath this *man* this wisdom, and *these* mighty works?

13:55 Is not this the carpenter's son? is not his mother called Mary? and his brethren, James, and Joses, and Simon, and Judas?

13:56 And his sisters, are they not all with us? Whence then hath this *man* all these things?

13:57 And they were offended in him. But Jesus said unto them, A prophet is not without honour, save in his own country, and in his own house.

13:58 And he did not many mighty works there because of their unbelief.

CHAPTER FOURTEEN

14:1 At that time Herod the tetrarch heard of the fame of Jesus,

14:2 And said unto his servants, This is John the Baptist; he is risen from the dead; and therefore mighty works do shew forth themselves in him.

14:3 For Herod had laid hold on John, and bound him, and put *him* in prison for Herodias' sake, his brother Philip's wife.

14:4 For John said unto him, It is not lawful for thee to have her.

14:5 And when he would have put him to death, he feared the multitude, because they counted him as a prophet.

14:6 But when Herod's birthday was kept, the daughter of Herodias danced before them, and pleased Herod.

14:7 Whereupon he promised with an oath to give her whatsoever she would ask.

14:8 And she, being before instructed of her mother, said, Give me here John Baptist's head in a charger.

14:9 And the king was sorry: nevertheless for the oath's sake, and them which sat with him at meat, he commanded *it* to be given *her.*

14:10 And he sent, and beheaded John in the prison.

14:11 And his head was brought in a charger, and given to the damsel: and she brought *it* to her mother.

14:12 And his disciples came, and took up the body, and buried it, and went and told Jesus.

14:13 When Jesus heard *of it,* he departed thence by ship into a desert place apart: and when the people had heard *thereof,* they followed him on foot out of the cities.

14:14 And Jesus went forth, and saw a great multitude, and was moved with compassion toward them, and he healed their sick.

14:15 And when it was evening, his disciples came to him, saying, This is a desert place, and the time is now past; send the multitude away, that they may go into the villages, and buy themselves victuals.

14:16 But Jesus said unto them, They need not depart; give ye them to eat.

14:17 And they say unto him, We have here but five loaves, and two fishes.

14:18 He said, Bring them hither to me.

14:19 And he commanded the multitude to sit down on the grass, and took the five loaves, and the two fishes, and looking up to heaven, he blessed, and brake, and gave the loaves to *his* disciples, and the disciples to the multitude.

14:20 And they did all eat, and were filled: and they took up of the fragments that remained twelve baskets full.

14:21 And they that had eaten were about five thousand men, beside women and children.

14:22 And straightway Jesus constrained his disciples to get into a ship, and to go before him unto the other side, while he sent the multitudes away.

14:23 And when he had sent the multitudes away, he went up into a mountain apart to pray: and when the evening was come, he was there alone.

14:24 But the ship was now in the midst of the sea, tossed with waves: for the wind was contrary.

14:25 And in the fourth watch of the night Jesus went unto them, walking on the sea.

14:26 And when the disciples saw him walking on the sea, they were troubled, saying, It is a spirit; and they cried out for fear.

14:27 But straightway Jesus spake unto them, saying, Be of good cheer; it is I; be not afraid.

14:28 And Peter answered him and said, Lord, if it be thou, bid me come unto thee on the water.

14:29 And he said, Come. And when Peter was come down out of the ship, he walked on the water, to go to Jesus.

14:30 But when he saw the wind boisterous, he was afraid; and beginning to sink, he cried, saying, Lord, save me.

14:31 And immediately Jesus stretched forth *his* hand, and caught him, and said unto him, O thou of little faith, wherefore didst thou doubt?

14:32 And when they were come into the ship, the wind ceased.

14:33 Then they that were in the ship came and worshipped him, saying, Of a truth thou art the Son of God.

14:34 And when they were gone over, they came into the land of Gennesaret.

14:35 And when the men of that place had knowledge of him, they sent out into all that country round about, and brought unto him all that were diseased;

14:36 And besought him that they might only touch the hem of his garment: and as many as touched were made perfectly whole.

CHAPTER FIFTEEN

15:1 Then came to Jesus scribes and Pharisees, which were of Jerusalem, saying,

15:2 Why do thy disciples transgress the tradition of the elders? for they wash not their hands when they eat bread.

15:3 But he answered and said unto them, Why do ye also transgress the commandment of God by your tradition?

15:4 For God commanded, saying, Honour thy father and mother: and, He that curseth father or mother, let him die the death.

15:5 But ye say, Whosoever shall say to *his* father or *his* mother, *It is* a gift, by whatsoever thou mightest be profited by me;

15:6 And honour not his father or his mother, *he shall be free.* Thus have ye made the commandment of God of none effect by your tradition.

15:7 *Ye* hypocrites, well did Esaias prophesy of you, saying,

15:8 This people draweth nigh unto me with their mouth,

and honoureth me with *their* lips; but their heart is far from me.

15:9 But in vain they do worship me, teaching *for* doctrines the commandments of men.

15:10 And he called the multitude, and said unto them, Hear, and understand:

15:11 Not that which goeth into the mouth defileth a man; but that which cometh out of the mouth, this defileth a man.

15:12 Then came his disciples, and said unto him, Knowest thou that the Pharisees were offended, after they heard this saying?

15:13 But he answered and said, Every plant, which my heavenly Father hath not planted, shall be rooted up.

15:14 Let them alone: they be blind leaders of the blind. And if the blind lead the blind, both shall fall into the ditch.

15:15 Then answered Peter and said unto him, Declare unto us this parable.

15:16 And Jesus said, Are ye also yet without understanding?

15:17 Do not ye yet understand, that whatsoever entereth in at the mouth goeth into the belly, and is cast out into the draught?

15:18 But those things which proceed out of the mouth come forth from the heart; and they defile the man.

15:19 For out of the heart proceed evil thoughts, murders, adulteries, fornications, thefts, false witness, blasphemies:

15:20 These are *the things* which defile a man: but to eat with unwashen hands defileth not a man.

15:21 Then Jesus went thence, and departed into the coasts of Tyre and Sidon.

15:22 And, behold, a woman of Canaan came out of the same coasts, and cried unto him, saying, Have mercy on me, O Lord, *thou* Son of David; my daughter is grievously vexed with a devil.

15:23 But he answered her not a word. And his disciples came and besought him, saying, Send her away; for she crieth after us.

15:24 But he answered and said, I am not sent but unto the lost sheep of the house of Israel.

15:25 Then came she and worshipped him, saying, Lord, help me.

15:26 But he answered and said, It is not meet to take the children's bread, and to cast *it* to dogs.

15:27 And she said, Truth, Lord: yet the dogs eat of the crumbs which fall from their masters' table.

15:28 Then Jesus answered and said unto her, O woman, great *is* thy faith: be it unto thee even as thou wilt. And her daughter was made whole from that very hour.

15:29 And Jesus departed from thence, and came nigh unto the sea of Galilee; and went up into a mountain, and sat down there.

15:30 And great multitudes came unto him, having with them *those that were* lame, blind, dumb, maimed, and many others, and cast them down at Jesus' feet; and he healed them:

15:31 Insomuch that the multitude wondered, when they saw the dumb to speak, the maimed to be whole, the lame to walk, and the blind to see: and they glorified the God of Israel.

15:32 Then Jesus called his disciples *unto him,* and said, I have compassion on the multitude, because they continue with me now three days, and have nothing to eat: and I will not send them away fasting, lest they faint in the way.

15:33 And his disciples say unto him, Whence should we have so much bread in the wilderness, as to fill so great a multitude?

15:34 And Jesus saith unto them, How many loaves have ye? And they said, Seven, and a few little fishes.

15:35 And he commanded the multitude to sit down on the ground.

15:36 And he took the seven loaves and the fishes, and gave thanks, and brake *them,* and gave to his disciples, and the disciples to the multitude.

15:37 And they did all eat, and were filled: and they took up of the broken *meat* that was left seven baskets full.

15:38 And they that did eat were four thousand men, beside women and children.

15:39 And he sent away the multitude, and took ship, and came into the coasts of Magdala.

CHAPTER SIXTEEN

16:1 The Pharisees also with the Sadducees came, and tempting desired him that he would shew them a sign from heaven.

16:2 He answered and said unto them, When it is evening, ye say, *It will be* fair weather: for the sky is red.

16:3 And in the morning, *It will be* foul weather to day: for the sky is red and lowring. O *ye* hypocrites, ye can discern the face of the sky; but can ye not *discern* the signs of the times?

People tend to believe the weather report but not God's Word.

16:4 A wicked and adulterous generation seeketh after a sign; and there shall no sign be given unto it, but the sign of the prophet Jonas. And he left them, and departed.

The Jewish people are represented in the Sacred Writings as married to the Most High; but they were often disloyal, forsaking their true husband and uniting themselves to Satan.

Jesus' statement, "sign after sign," implies that He knows that if He gives them another one they will only still demand further proof. He has already given them many signs, or proofs, that He is the Messiah and they still refuse to believe in Him, therefore only one more sign is necessary, the resurrection.

16:5 And when his disciples were come to the other side, they had forgotten to take bread.

16:6 Then Jesus said unto them, Take heed and beware of the leaven of the Pharisees and of the Sadducees.

Jesus compared false doctrine to yeast. It starts out small and insignificant but it grows and pollutes the whole lump.

16:7 And they reasoned among themselves, saying, *It is* because we have taken no bread.

16:8 *Which* when Jesus perceived, he said unto them, O ye of little faith, why reason ye among yourselves, because ye have brought no bread?

16:9 Do ye not yet understand, neither remember the five loaves of the five thousand, and how many baskets ye took up?

16:10 Neither the seven loaves of the four thousand, and how many baskets ye took up?

16:11 How is it that ye do not understand that I spake *it* not to you concerning bread, that ye should beware of the leaven of the Pharisees and of the Sadducees?

16:12 Then understood they how that he bade *them* not beware of the leaven of bread, but of the doctrine of the Pharisees and of the Sadducees.

16:13 When Jesus came into the coasts of Caesarea Philippi, he asked his disciples, saying, Whom do men say that I the Son of man am?

16:14 And they said, Some *say that thou art* John the Baptist: some, Elias; and others, Jeremias, or one of the prophets.

The crowd is confused about Jesus even today. Don't follow the crowd.

16:15 He saith unto them, But whom say ye that I am?

16:16 And Simon Peter answered and said, Thou art the Christ, the Son of the living God.

16:17 And Jesus answered and said unto him, Blessed art thou, Simon Barjona: for flesh and blood hath not revealed *it* unto thee, but my Father which is in heaven.

16:18 And I say also unto thee, That thou art Peter, and upon this rock I will build my church; and the gates of hell shall not prevail against it.

Peter means "a stone," a fragment of a rock. Jesus is "the Rock," see Psalm 118:22, Isaiah 28:16.

16:19 And I will give unto thee the keys of the kingdom of heaven: and whatsoever thou shalt bind on earth shall be bound in heaven: and whatsoever thou shalt loose on earth shall be loosed in heaven.

16:20 Then charged he his disciples that they should tell no man that he was Jesus the Christ.

16:21 From that time forth began Jesus to shew unto his disciples, how that he must go unto Jerusalem, and suffer many things of the elders and chief priests and scribes, and be killed, and be raised again the third day.

16:22 Then Peter took him, and began to rebuke him, saying, Be it far from thee, Lord: this shall not be unto thee.

Peter, the stone, became Peter the stumbling block. Every Christian is designated a "living stone" by the Sacred Writing and, like Peter, we can become stumbling stones if we are not careful to keep ourselves aligned with our Lord. Peter still did not understand what Jesus was doing.

16:23 But he turned, and said unto Peter, Get thee behind me, Satan: thou art an offence unto me: for thou savourest not the things that be of God, but those that be of men.

16:24 Then said Jesus unto his disciples, If any *man* will come after me, let him deny himself, and take up his cross, and follow me.

16:25 For whosoever will save his life shall lose it: and whosoever will lose his life for my sake shall find it.

16:26 For what is a man profited, if he shall gain the whole world, and lose his own soul? or what shall a man give in exchange for his soul?

16:27 For the Son of man shall come in the glory of his Father with his angels; and then he shall reward every man according to his works.

16:28 Verily I say unto you, There be some standing here, which shall not taste of death, till they see the Son of man coming in his kingdom.

CHAPTER SEVENTEEN

17:1 And after six days Jesus taketh Peter, James, and John his brother, and bringeth them up into an high mountain apart,

17:2 And was transfigured before them: and his face did shine as the sun, and his raiment was white as the light.

17:3 And, behold, there appeared unto them Moses and Elias talking with him.

17:4 Then answered Peter, and said unto Jesus, Lord, it is good for us to be here: if thou wilt, let us make here three tabernacles; one for thee, and one for Moses, and one for Elias.

17:5 While he yet spake, behold, a bright cloud overshadowed them: and behold a voice out of the cloud, which said, This is my beloved Son, in whom I am well pleased; hear ye him.

17:6 And when the disciples heard *it,* they fell on their face, and were sore afraid.

17:7 And Jesus came and touched them, and said, Arise,

and be not afraid.

17:8 And when they had lifted up their eyes, they saw no man, save Jesus only.

17:9 And as they came down from the mountain, Jesus charged them, saying, Tell the vision to no man, until the Son of man be risen again from the dead.

17:10 And his disciples asked him, saying, Why then say the scribes that Elias must first come?

17:11 And Jesus answered and said unto them, Elias truly shall first come, and restore all things.

17:12 But I say unto you, That Elias is come already, and they knew him not, but have done unto him whatsoever they listed. Likewise shall also the Son of man suffer of them

17:13 Then the disciples understood that he spake unto them of John the Baptist.

17:14 And when they were come to the multitude, there came to him a *certain* man, kneeling down to him, and saying,

17:15 Lord, have mercy on my son: for he is lunatick, and sore vexed: for ofttimes he falleth into the fire, and oft into the water.

17:16 And I brought him to thy disciples, and they could not cure him.

17:17 Then Jesus answered and said, O faithless and perverse generation, how long shall I be with you? how long shall I suffer you? bring him hither to me.

17:18 And Jesus rebuked the devil; and he departed out of

him: and the child was cured from that very hour.

17:19 Then came the disciples to Jesus apart, and said, Why could not we cast him out?

17:20 And Jesus said unto them, Because of your unbelief: for verily I say unto you, If ye have faith as a grain of mustard seed, ye shall say unto this mountain, Remove hence to yonder place; and it shall remove; and nothing shall be impossible unto you.

17:21 Howbeit this kind goeth not out but by prayer and fasting.

17:22 And while they abode in Galilee, Jesus said unto them, The Son of man shall be betrayed into the hands of men:

17:23 And they shall kill him, and the third day he shall be raised again. And they were exceeding sorry.

17:24 And when they were come to Capernaum, they that received tribute *money* came to Peter, and said, Doth not your master pay tribute?

17:25 He saith, Yes. And when he was come into the house, Jesus prevented him, saying, What thinkest thou, Simon? of whom do the kings of the earth take custom or tribute? of their own children, or of strangers?

17:26 Peter saith unto him, Of strangers. Jesus saith unto him, Then are the children free.

17:27 Notwithstanding, lest we should offend them, go thou to the sea, and cast an hook, and take up the fish that first cometh up; and when thou hast opened his mouth, thou shalt find a piece of money: that take, and give unto them for me and thee.

CHAPTER EIGHTEEN

18:1 At the same time came the disciples unto Jesus, saying, Who is the greatest in the kingdom of heaven?

18:2 And Jesus called a little child unto him, and set him in the midst of them,

18:3 And said, Verily I say unto you, Except ye be converted, and become as little children, ye shall not enter into the kingdom of heaven.

18:4 Whosoever therefore shall humble himself as this little child, the same is greatest in the kingdom of heaven.

18:5 And whoso shall receive one such little child in my name receiveth me.

18:6 But whoso shall offend one of these little ones which believe in me, it were better for him that a millstone were hanged about his neck, and *that* he were drowned in the depth of the sea.

18:7 Woe unto the world because of offences! for it must needs be that offences come; but woe to that man by whom the offence cometh!

18:8 Wherefore if thy hand or thy foot offend thee, cut them off, and cast *them* from thee: it is better for thee to enter into life halt or maimed, rather than having two hands or two feet to be cast into everlasting fire.

18:9 And if thine eye offend thee, pluck it out, and cast *it* from thee: it is better for thee to enter into life with one eye, rather than having two eyes to be cast into hell fire.

18:10 Take heed that ye despise not one of these little ones; for I say unto you, That in heaven their angels do always behold the face of my Father which is in heaven.

18:11 For the Son of man is come to save that which was lost.

18:12 How think ye? if a man have an hundred sheep, and one of them be gone astray, doth he not leave the ninety and nine, and goeth into the mountains, and seeketh that which is gone astray?

18:13 And if so be that he find it, verily I say unto you, he rejoiceth more of that *sheep,* than of the ninety and nine which went not astray.

18:14 Even so it is not the will of your Father which is in heaven, that one of these little ones should perish.

18:15 Moreover if thy brother shall trespass against thee, go and tell him his fault between thee and him alone: if he shall hear thee, thou hast gained thy brother.

18:16 But if he will not hear *thee, then* take with thee one or two more, that in the mouth of two or three witnesses every word may be established.

18:17 And if he shall neglect to hear them, tell *it* unto the church: but if he neglect to hear the church, let him be unto thee as an heathen man and a publican.

18:18 Verily I say unto you, Whatsoever ye shall bind on earth shall be bound in heaven: and whatsoever ye shall loose on earth shall be loosed in heaven.

18:19 Again I say unto you, That if two of you shall agree on earth as touching any thing that they shall ask, it shall be done for them of my Father which is in heaven.

18:20 For where two or three are gathered together in my name, there am I in the midst of them.

18:21 Then came Peter to him, and said, Lord, how oft shall my brother sin against me, and I forgive him? till seven times?

18:22 Jesus saith unto him, I say not unto thee, Until seven times: but, Until seventy times seven.

18:23 Therefore is the kingdom of heaven likened unto a certain king, which would take account of his servants.

18:24 And when he had begun to reckon, one was brought unto him, which owed him ten thousand talents.

18:25 But forasmuch as he had not to pay, his lord commanded him to be sold, and his wife, and children, and all that he had, and payment to be made.

18:26 The servant therefore fell down, and worshipped him, saying, Lord, have patience with me, and I will pay thee all.

18:27 Then the lord of that servant was moved with compassion, and loosed him, and forgave him the debt.

18:28 But the same servant went out, and found one of his

fellowservants, which owed him an hundred pence: and he laid hands on him, and took *him* by the throat, saying, Pay me that thou owest.

18:29 And his fellowservant fell down at his feet, and besought him, saying, Have patience with me, and I will pay thee all.

18:30 And he would not: but went and cast him into prison, till he should pay the debt.

18:31 So when his fellowservants saw what was done, they were very sorry, and came and told unto their lord all that was done.

18:32 Then his lord, after that he had called him, said unto him, O thou wicked servant, I forgave thee all that debt, because thou desiredst me:

18:33 Shouldest not thou also have had compassion on thy fellowservant, even as I had pity on thee?

18:34 And his lord was wroth, and delivered him to the tormentors, till he should pay all that was due unto him.

18:35 So likewise shall my heavenly Father do also unto you, if ye from your hearts forgive not every one his brother their trespasses.

CHAPTER NINETEEN

19:1 And it came to pass, *that* when Jesus had finished these sayings, he departed from Galilee, and came into the coasts of Judaea beyond Jordan;

19:2 And great multitudes followed him; and he healed them there.

19:3 The Pharisees also came unto him, tempting him, and saying unto him, Is it lawful for a man to put away his wife for every cause?

19:4 And he answered and said unto them, Have ye not read, that he which made *them* at the beginning made them male and female,

19:5 And said, For this cause shall a man leave father and mother, and shall cleave to his wife: and they twain shall be one flesh?

19:6 Wherefore they are no more twain, but one flesh. What therefore God hath joined together, let not man put asunder.

19:7 They say unto him, Why did Moses then command to give a writing of divorcement, and to put her away?

19:8 He saith unto them, Moses because of the hardness of your hearts suffered you to put away your wives: but from the beginning it was not so.

19:9 And I say unto you, Whosoever shall put away his wife, except *it be* for fornication, and shall marry another, committeth adultery: and whoso marrieth her which is put away doth commit adultery.

19:10 His disciples say unto him, If the case of the man be so with *his* wife, it is not good to marry.

19:11 But he said unto them, All *men* cannot receive this saying, save *they* to whom it is given.

19:12 For there are some eunuchs, which were so born from *their* mother's womb: and there are some eunuchs, which were made eunuchs of men: and there be eunuchs, which have made themselves eunuchs for the kingdom of heaven's sake. He that is able to receive *it,* let him receive *it.*

19:13 Then were there brought unto him little children, that he should put *his* hands on them, and pray: and the disciples rebuked them.

19:14 But Jesus said, Suffer little children, and forbid them not, to come unto me: for of such is the kingdom of heaven.

19:15 And he laid *his* hands on them, and departed thence.

19:16 And, behold, one came and said unto him, Good Master, what good thing shall I do, that I may have eternal life?

19:17 And he said unto him, Why callest thou me good? *there is* none good but one, *that is,* God: but if thou wilt enter into life, keep the commandments.

19:18 He saith unto him, Which? Jesus said, Thou shalt do no murder, Thou shalt not commit adultery, Thou shalt not steal, Thou shalt not bear false witness,

19:19 Honour thy father and *thy* mother: and, Thou shalt love thy neighbour as thyself.

19:20 The young man saith unto him, All these things have I kept from my youth up: what lack I yet?

19:21 Jesus said unto him, If thou wilt be perfect, go *and* sell that thou hast, and give to the poor, and thou shalt have treasure in heaven: and come *and* follow me.

19:22 But when the young man heard that saying, he went away sorrowful: for he had great possessions.

19:23 Then said Jesus unto his disciples, Verily I say unto you, That a rich man shall hardly enter into the kingdom of heaven.

19:24 And again I say unto you, It is easier for a camel to go through the eye of a needle, than for a rich man to enter into the kingdom of God.

19:25 When his disciples heard *it,* they were exceedingly amazed, saying, Who then can be saved?

19:26 But Jesus beheld *them,* and said unto them, With men this is impossible; but with God all things are possible.

19:27 Then answered Peter and said unto him, Behold, we have forsaken all, and followed thee; what shall we have therefore?

19:28 And Jesus said unto them, Verily I say unto you, That ye which have followed me, in the regeneration when the

Son of man shall sit in the throne of his glory, ye also shall sit upon twelve thrones, judging the twelve tribes of Israel.

19:29 And every one that hath forsaken houses, or brethren, or sisters, or father, or mother, or wife, or children, or lands, for my name's sake, shall receive an hundredfold, and shall inherit everlasting life.

19:30 But many *that are* first shall be last; and the last *shall be* first.

CHAPTER TWENTY

20:1 For the kingdom of heaven is like unto a man *that is* an householder, which went out early in the morning to hire labourers into his vineyard.

20:2 And when he had agreed with the labourers for a penny a day, he sent them into his vineyard.

20:3 And he went out about the third hour, and saw others standing idle in the marketplace,

20:4 And said unto them; Go ye also into the vineyard, and whatsoever is right I will give you. And they went their way.

20:5 Again he went out about the sixth and ninth hour, and did likewise.

20:6 And about the eleventh hour he went out, and found others standing idle, and saith unto them, Why stand ye here all the day idle?

20:7 They say unto him, Because no man hath hired us. He saith unto them, Go ye also into the vineyard; and whatsoever is right, *that* shall ye receive.

20:8 So when even was come, the lord of the vineyard saith unto his steward, Call the labourers, and give them *their* hire, beginning from the last unto the first.

20:9 And when they came that *were hired* about the eleventh hour, they received every man a penny.

20:10 But when the first came, they supposed that they should have received more; and they likewise received every man a penny.

20:11 And when they had received *it,* they murmured against the goodman of the house,

20:12 Saying, These last have wrought *but* one hour, and thou hast made them equal unto us, which have borne the burden and heat of the day.

20:13 But he answered one of them, and said, Friend, I do thee no wrong: didst not thou agree with me for a penny?

20:14 Take *that* thine *is,* and go thy way: I will give unto this last, even as unto thee.

20:15 Is it not lawful for me to do what I will with mine own? Is thine eye evil, because I am good?

20:16 So the last shall be first, and the first last: for many be called, but few chosen.

20:17 And Jesus going up to Jerusalem took the twelve disciples apart in the way, and said unto them,

20:18 Behold, we go up to Jerusalem; and the Son of man shall be betrayed unto the chief priests and unto the scribes, and they shall condemn him to death,

20:19 And shall deliver him to the Gentiles to mock, and to scourge, and to crucify *him:* and the third day he shall rise again.

20:20 Then came to him the mother of Zebedee's children with her sons, worshipping *him,* and desiring a certain thing of him.

20:21 And he said unto her, What wilt thou? She saith unto him, Grant that these my two sons may sit, the one on thy right hand, and the other on the left, in thy kingdom.

20:22 But Jesus answered and said, Ye know not what ye ask. Are ye able to drink of the cup that I shall drink of, and to be baptized with the baptism that I am baptized with? They say unto him, We are able.

20:23 And he saith unto them, Ye shall drink indeed of my cup, and be baptized with the baptism that I am baptized with: but to sit on my right hand, and on my left, is not mine to give, but *it shall be given to them* for whom it is prepared of my Father.

20:24 And when the ten heard *it,* they were moved with indignation against the two brethren.

20:25 But Jesus called them *unto him,* and said, Ye know that the princes of the Gentiles exercise dominion over them, and they that are great exercise authority upon them.

20:26 But it shall not be so among you: but whosoever will be great among you, let him be your minister;

20:27 And whosoever will be chief among you, let him be your servant:

20:28 Even as the Son of man came not to be ministered unto, but to minister, and to give his life a ransom for many.

20:29 And as they departed from Jericho, a great multitude followed him.

20:30 And, behold, two blind men sitting by the way side, when they heard that Jesus passed by, cried out, saying, Have mercy on us, O Lord, *thou* Son of David.

20:31 And the multitude rebuked them, because they should hold their peace: but they cried the more, saying, Have mercy on us, O Lord, *thou* Son of David.

20:32 And Jesus stood still, and called them, and said, What will ye that I shall do unto you?

20:33 They say unto him, Lord, that our eyes may be opened.

20:34 So Jesus had compassion *on them,* and touched their eyes: and immediately their eyes received sight, and they followed him.

CHAPTER TWENTY ONE

21:1 And when they drew nigh unto Jerusalem, and were come to Bethphage, unto the mount of Olives, then sent Jesus two disciples,

21:2 Saying unto them, Go into the village over against you, and straightway ye shall find an ass tied, and a colt with her: loose *them,* and bring *them* unto me.

21:3 And if any *man* say ought unto you, ye shall say, The Lord hath need of them; and straightway he will send them.

21:4 All this was done, that it might be fulfilled which was spoken by the prophet, saying,

21:5 Tell ye the daughter of Sion, Behold, thy King cometh unto thee, meek, and sitting upon an ass, and a colt the foal of an ass.

21:6 And the disciples went, and did as Jesus commanded them,

21:7 And brought the ass, and the colt, and put on them their clothes, and they set *him* thereon.

21:8 And a very great multitude spread their garments in the way; others cut down branches from the trees, and strawed *them* in the way.

21:9 And the multitudes that went before, and that followed, cried, saying, Hosanna to the Son of David: Blessed *is* he that cometh in the name of the Lord; Hosanna in the highest.

21:10 And when he was come into Jerusalem, all the city was moved, saying, Who is this?

21:11 And the multitude said, This is Jesus the prophet of Nazareth of Galilee.

21:12 And Jesus went into the temple of God, and cast out all them that sold and bought in the temple, and overthrew the tables of the moneychangers, and the seats of them that sold doves,

21:13 And said unto them, It is written, My house shall be called the house of prayer; but ye have made it a den of thieves.

21:14 And the blind and the lame came to him in the temple; and he healed them.

21:15 And when the chief priests and scribes saw the wonderful things that he did, and the children crying in the temple, and saying, Hosanna to the Son of David; they were sore displeased,

21:16 And said unto him, Hearest thou what these say? And Jesus saith unto them, Yea; have ye never read, Out of the mouth of babes and sucklings thou hast perfected praise?

21:17 And he left them, and went out of the city into Bethany; and he lodged there.

21:18 Now in the morning as he returned into the city, he hungered.

21:19 And when he saw a fig tree in the way, he came to it, and found nothing thereon, but leaves only, and said unto it, Let no fruit grow on thee henceforward for ever. And presently the fig tree withered away.

21:20 And when the disciples saw *it,* they marvelled, saying, How soon is the fig tree withered away!

21:21 Jesus answered and said unto them, Verily I say unto you, If ye have faith, and doubt not, ye shall not only do this *which is done* to the fig tree, but also if ye shall say unto this mountain, Be thou removed, and be thou cast into the sea; it shall be done.

21:22 And all things, whatsoever ye shall ask in prayer, believing, ye shall receive.

21:23 And when he was come into the temple, the chief priests and the elders of the people came unto him as he was teaching, and said, By what authority doest thou these things? and who gave thee this authority?

21:24 And Jesus answered and said unto them, I also will ask you one thing, which if ye tell me, I in like wise will tell you by what authority I do these things.

21:25 The baptism of John, whence was it? from heaven, or of men? And they reasoned with themselves, saying, If we shall say, From heaven; he will say unto us, Why did ye not then believe him?

21:26 But if we shall say, Of men; we fear the people; for all hold John as a prophet.

21:27 And they answered Jesus, and said, We cannot tell. And he said unto them, Neither tell I you by what authority I do these things.

21:28 But what think ye? A *certain* man had two sons; and he came to the first, and said, Son, go work to day in my vineyard.

21:29 He answered and said, I will not: but afterward he repented, and went.

21:30 And he came to the second, and said likewise. And he answered and said, I *go,* sir: and went not.

21:31 Whether of them twain did the will of *his* father? They say unto him, The first. Jesus saith unto them, Verily I say unto you, That the publicans and the harlots go into the kingdom of God before you.

21:32 For John came unto you in the way of righteousness, and ye believed him not: but the publicans and the harlots believed him: and ye, when ye had seen *it,* repented not afterward, that ye might believe him.

21:33 Hear another parable: There was a certain householder, which planted a vineyard, and hedged it round about, and digged a winepress in it, and built a tower, and let it out to husbandmen, and went into a far country:

21:34 And when the time of the fruit drew near, he sent his servants to the husbandmen, that they might receive the fruits of it.

21:35 And the husbandmen took his servants, and beat one, and killed another, and stoned another.

21:36 Again, he sent other servants more than the first: and they did unto them likewise.

21:37 But last of all he sent unto them his son, saying, They will reverence my son.

21:38 But when the husbandmen saw the son, they said among themselves, This is the heir; come, let us kill him, and let us seize on his inheritance.

21:39 And they caught him, and cast *him* out of the vineyard, and slew *him.*

21:40 When the lord therefore of the vineyard cometh, what will he do unto those husbandmen?

21:41 They say unto him, He will miserably destroy those wicked men, and will let out *his* vineyard unto other husbandmen, which shall render him the fruits in their seasons.

21:42 Jesus saith unto them, Did ye never read in the scriptures, The stone which the builders rejected, the same is become the head of the corner: this is the Lord's doing, and it is marvellous in our eyes?

21:43 Therefore say I unto you, The kingdom of God shall be taken from you, and given to a nation bringing forth the fruits thereof.

21:44 And whosoever shall fall on this stone shall be broken: but on whomsoever it shall fall, it will grind him to powder.

21:45 And when the chief priests and Pharisees had heard his parables, they perceived that he spake of them.

21:46 But when they sought to lay hands on him, they

feared the multitude, because they took him for a prophet.

CHAPTER TWENTY TWO

22:1 And Jesus answered and spake unto them again by parables, and said,

22:2 The kingdom of heaven is like unto a certain king, which made a marriage for his son,

22:3 And sent forth his servants to call them that were bidden to the wedding: and they would not come.

22:4 Again, he sent forth other servants, saying, Tell them which are bidden, Behold, I have prepared my dinner: my oxen and *my* fatlings *are* killed, and all things *are* ready: come unto the marriage.

22:5 But they made light of *it,* and went their ways, one to his farm, another to his merchandise:

22:6 And the remnant took his servants, and entreated *them* spitefully, and slew *them.*

22:7 But when the king heard *thereof,* he was wroth: and he sent forth his armies, and destroyed those murderers, and burned up their city.

22:8 Then saith he to his servants, The wedding is ready, but they which were bidden were not worthy.

22:9 Go ye therefore into the highways, and as many as ye shall find, bid to the marriage.

22:10 So those servants went out into the highways, and gathered together all as many as they found, both bad and good: and the wedding was furnished with guests.

22:11 And when the king came in to see the guests, he saw there a man which had not on a wedding garment:

22:12 And he saith unto him, Friend, how camest thou in hither not having a wedding garment? And he was speechless.

22:13 Then said the king to the servants, Bind him hand and foot, and take him away, and cast *him* into outer darkness; there shall be weeping and gnashing of teeth.

22:14 For many are called, but few *are* chosen.

22:15 Then went the Pharisees, and took counsel how they might entangle him in *his* talk.

22:16 And they sent out unto him their disciples with the Herodians, saying, Master, we know that thou art true, and teachest the way of God in truth, neither carest thou for any *man:* for thou regardest not the person of men.

22:17 Tell us therefore, What thinkest thou? Is it lawful to give tribute unto Caesar, or not?

22:18 But Jesus perceived their wickedness, and said, Why tempt ye me, *ye* hypocrites?

22:19 Shew me the tribute money. And they brought unto

him a penny.

22:20 And he saith unto them, Whose *is* this image and superscription?

22:21 They say unto him, Caesar's. Then saith he unto them, Render therefore unto Caesar the things which are Caesar's; and unto God the things that are God's.

22:22 When they had heard *these words,* they marvelled, and left him, and went their way.

22:23 The same day came to him the Sadducees, which say that there is no resurrection, and asked him,

   That's why they were "Sad, you see."

22:24 Saying, Master, Moses said, If a man die, having no children, his brother shall marry his wife, and raise up seed unto his brother.

   This law is found in Deuteronomy 25:5. That law's purpose was that the children produced by this marriage should be counted in the genealogy of the deceased brother and receive his estate. The Hindus have a similar law and for the same reason.

22:25 Now there were with us seven brethren: and the first, when he had married a wife, died, and, having no issue, left his wife unto his brother:

22:26 Likewise the second also, and the third, unto the seventh.

22:27 And last of all the woman died also.

22:28 Therefore in the resurrection whose wife shall she be of the seven? for they all had her.

Some Rabbis taught, that if a woman had two husbands in this world she would have the first only restored to her in the world to come.

The question put by these men is well suited to the mouth of a libertine. Those who live without God in this world have no other god than this world. The stream does not rise higher than the spring.

These men and their brethren, the ones who reject The Law and religious restraint, the atheists, and the deists, and others like them, cannot comprehend heaven as a place of blessedness unless they can hope to find in it the gratification of their self-centered desires and lusts. Mohammad built his paradise on such flawed ground.

22:29 Jesus answered and said unto them, Ye do err, not knowing the scriptures, nor the power of God.

22:30 For in the resurrection they neither marry, nor are given in marriage, but are as the angels of God in heaven.

22:31 But as touching the resurrection of the dead, have ye not read that which was spoken unto you by God, saying,

22:32 I am the God of Abraham, and the God of Isaac, and the God of Jacob? God is not the God of the dead, but of the living.

22:33 And when the multitude heard *this,* they were astonished at his doctrine.

22:34 But when the Pharisees had heard that he had put the Sadducees to silence, they were gathered together.

22:35 Then one of them, *which was* a lawyer, asked *him a question,* tempting him, and saying,

22:36 Master, which *is* the great commandment in the law?

22:37 Jesus said unto him, Thou shalt love the Lord thy God with all thy heart, and with all thy soul, and with all thy mind.

22:38 This is the first and great commandment.

22:39 And the second *is* like unto it, Thou shalt love thy neighbour as thyself.

22:40 On these two commandments hang all the law and the prophets.

22:41 While the Pharisees were gathered together, Jesus asked them,

22:42 Saying, What think ye of Christ? whose son is he? They say unto him, *The Son* of David.

22:43 He saith unto them, How then doth David in spirit call him Lord, saying,

22:44 The LORD said unto my Lord, Sit thou on my right hand, till I make thine enemies thy footstool?

22:45 If David then call him Lord, how is he his son?

22:46 And no man was able to answer him a word, neither durst any *man* from that day forth ask him any more *questions.*

    All those in leadership positions who have chosen to oppose Jesus are now trying to hide in the shadows and wait for a more opportune time. Now we see Jesus demonstrating that not only does He know how to answer their questions well He is quite capable of bringing up questions which are beyond their ability or actual willingness to accurately answer. The way this question was presented indicated to them that not only did He know the answer but He was prepared to back up His claim. They, of course, would not have liked His answer. They had, after all, attempted to stone Him before when He had attempted to clearly reveal to them Who He is. Some of the people in the crowd would not have liked the answer either. His followers, however, know and embrace that answer's truth.

Jesus showed how weak and defective the Scribes were in their preaching, and how unable to solve the difficulties that occurred in the Scripture which they undertook to expound upon. Matthew fleshed out this challenge from Jesus more clearly than Peter did in his Gospel account because Matthew's intended audience is the Jewish people. They, the Jewish religious leadership, had added in various explanations and traditions to cover up their lack of understanding and when successfully challenged on their explanations, instead of going back to the drawing board, they had simply added additional explanations to their explanations. Therefore just like a math problem where a small error had occurred early in the problem solving process the work had gone on and the error was compounded instead of corrected.

The caution Jesus gave the people to beware of those practicing error.

Satan's greatest weapon is ignorance of God's Word. A right knowledge of the Scripture is the best preventative and preservative against error. Keep the truth, the Scriptural truth, and it shall keep thee.

Those who stand outside the Church and claim all

churches are corrupt are also possessed of the same spirit as the Sadducees, at best, and/or of the Herodians and Pharisees. Those individuals seem to like to criticize and belittle the church and all of those who attend them on a regular basis. Although they seldom, if ever, read the Bible they frequently exhibit a tendency to claim superior knowledge regarding The Holy Bible's contents and what it all means than those who are actually far more carefully studying the Scripture and trying to accurately comprehend the voice of God found therein.

In America, those who never enter into a church apart from a wedding or a funeral still receive many blessings because of the existence of the church. And when they rail against the church they are doing long-term damage to themselves and much of what they hold dear which, unfortunately, they may not comprehend until it is too late.

Refusing to go to Church because there might be "hypocrites" in that place is very similar to refusing to go to the gym because there might be "out of shape people" in that place. The church is a lot like Noah's ark: Sometimes it stinks, but if you get out you drown.

CHAPTER TENTY THREE

23:1 Then spake Jesus to the multitude, and to his disciples,

23:2 Saying, The scribes and the Pharisees sit in Moses' seat:

23:3 All therefore whatsoever they bid you observe, *that* observe and do; but do not ye after their works: for they say, and do not.

Take notice, Jesus has not given you permission to not go to church.

23:4 For they bind heavy burdens and grievous to be borne, and lay *them* on men's shoulders; but they *themselves* will not move them with one of their fingers.

23:5 But all their works they do for to be seen of men: they make broad their phylacteries, and enlarge the borders of their garments,

23:6 And love the uppermost rooms at feasts, and the chief seats in the synagogues,

23:7 And greetings in the markets, and to be called of men, Rabbi, Rabbi.

23:8 But be not ye called Rabbi: for one is your Master, *even* Christ; and all ye are brethren.

23:9 And call no *man* your father upon the earth: for one is your Father, which is in heaven.

23:10 Neither be ye called masters: for one is your Master, *even* Christ.

23:11 But he that is greatest among you shall be your servant.

23:12 And whosoever shall exalt himself shall be abased; and he that shall humble himself shall be exalted.

23:13 But woe unto you, scribes and Pharisees, hypocrites! for ye shut up the kingdom of heaven against men: for ye neither go in *yourselves,* neither suffer ye them that are entering to go in.

23:14 Woe unto you, scribes and Pharisees, hypocrites! for ye devour widows' houses, and for a pretence make long prayer: therefore ye shall receive the greater damnation.

23:15 Woe unto you, scribes and Pharisees, hypocrites! for ye compass sea and land to make one proselyte, and when he is made, ye make him twofold more the child of hell than yourselves.

23:16 Woe unto you, *ye* blind guides, which say, Whosoever shall swear by the temple, it is nothing; but whosoever shall swear by the gold of the temple, he is a debtor!

23:17 *Ye* fools and blind: for whether is greater, the gold, or the temple that sanctifieth the gold?

23:18 And, Whosoever shall swear by the altar, it is nothing; but whosoever sweareth by the gift that is upon it, he is guilty.

23:19 *Ye* fools and blind: for whether *is* greater, the gift, or the altar that sanctifieth the gift?

23:20 Whoso therefore shall swear by the altar, sweareth by it, and by all things thereon.

23:21 And whoso shall swear by the temple, sweareth by it, and by Him that dwelleth therein.

23:22 And he that shall swear by heaven, sweareth by the throne of God, and by him that sitteth thereon.

23:23 Woe unto you, scribes and Pharisees, hypocrites! for ye pay tithe of mint and anise and cummin, and have omitted the weightier *matters* of the law, judgment, mercy, and faith: these ought ye to have done, and not to leave the other undone.

23:24 *Ye* blind guides, which strain at a gnat, and swallow a camel.

23:25 Woe unto you, scribes and Pharisees, hypocrites! for ye make clean the outside of the cup and of the platter, but within they are full of extortion and excess.

23:26 *Thou* blind Pharisee, cleanse first that *which is* within the cup and platter, that the outside of them may be clean also.

23:27 Woe unto you, scribes and Pharisees, hypocrites! for

ye are like unto whited sepulchres, which indeed appear beautiful outward, but are within full of dead *men's* bones, and of all uncleanness.

23:28 Even so ye also outwardly appear righteous unto men, but within ye are full of hypocrisy and iniquity.

23:29 Woe unto you, scribes and Pharisees, hypocrites! because ye build the tombs of the prophets, and garnish the sepulchres of the righteous,

23:30 And say, If we had been in the days of our fathers, we would not have been partakers with them in the blood of the prophets.

23:31 Wherefore ye be witnesses unto yourselves, that ye are the children of them which killed the prophets.

23:32 Fill ye up then the measure of your fathers.

23:33 *Ye* serpents, *ye* generation of vipers, how can ye escape the damnation of hell?

23:34 Wherefore, behold, I send unto you prophets, and wise men, and scribes: and *some* of them ye shall kill and crucify; and *some* of them shall ye scourge in your synagogues, and persecute *them* from city to city:

23:35 That upon you may come all the righteous blood shed upon the earth, from the blood of righteous Abel unto the blood of Zacharias son of Barachias, whom ye slew between the temple and the altar.

23:36 Verily I say unto you, All these things shall come upon this generation.

23:37 O Jerusalem, Jerusalem, *thou* that killest the

prophets, and stonest them which are sent unto thee, how often would I have gathered thy children together, even as a hen gathereth her chickens under *her* wings, and ye would not!

23:38 Behold, your house is left unto you desolate.

He means the temple. Once it was God's temple, God's own house, but now Jesus is implying that God is abandoning it.

23:39 For I say unto you, Ye shall not see me henceforth, till ye shall say, Blessed *is* he that cometh in the name of the Lord.

Jesus has just closed His last public discourse in the Temple and they were completely clueless; they should not have been. An incredible amount of evidence had been set before them but they still refused to see. There are always those who would rather blame holiness itself, than esteem it in those whom they do not like.

CHAPTER TWENTY FOUR

24:1 And Jesus went out, and departed from the temple: and his disciples came to *him* for to shew him the buildings of the temple.

> Or, And Jesus, going out of the temple, was going away. This is the arrangement of the words in several eminent manuscripts, versions, and fathers; and is much clearer than that in the common translation. The Jews say the temple was built of white and green-spotted marble. See Lightfoot. Josephus says the stones were white and strong; fifty feet long, twenty-four broad, and sixteen thick. Antiq. b. 15. c. xi. See Mar_13:1. – Adam Clarke

I strongly suspect that as Jesus departed the Temple this time he "shook the dust off of His feet." The disciples are staring at Jesus in wide-eyed wonder, having just witnessed the strong discourse given in the Temple and Jesus' demeanor as He now leaves the Temple

24:2 And Jesus said unto them, See ye not all these things? verily I say unto you, There shall not be left here one stone upon another, that shall not be thrown down.

The disciples were disturbed by Jesus' closing words in His final public discourse in the temple. They were expecting Him to set up His earthly kingdom and where could there possibly be a better place to set up His throne than in this magnificent place? Herod's Temple was one of the wonders of the world. Construction began about 20 B.C. and it was not yet complete when Jesus spoke these words. The historian Flavius Josephus tells us that from a distance it resembled a snow-covered mountain while the gold plating on the roof reflected the sun in a fiery splendor. Titus was unwilling to tear down so great a work as Herod's Temple and actually tried, several times during the siege, to prevent its destruction, but God had overruled him before the siege had ever begun.

Many have declared through the ages that Josephus must have greatly exaggerated its splendor but archeological digs have shown that his description was probably pretty accurate with little, if any, exaggeration (see Wars of the Jews, 5.5.1). "Six days battering at the walls, during the siege, made no impression upon them" – Wars of the Jews 6.4.1. That abomination called the Al-Aqsa Mosque is a shabby structure in comparison to Herod's Temple.

There are some who would like to date the synoptic gospels after A.D. 70 in order to void the predictive element involved with a before A.D. 45 publication. But that is an effort to limit the fore-knowledge of Jesus to a merely human basis, and perhaps, downplay the certainty of His second advent. However, internal evidences, properly understood, do not allow any portion of the New Testament to have been written after A.D. 69 with the exception of that portion called The Revelation.

24:3 And as he sat upon the mount of Olives, the disciples

came unto him privately, saying, Tell us, when shall these things be? and what *shall be* the sign of thy coming, and of the end of the world?

24:4 And Jesus answered and said unto them, Take heed that no man deceive you.

24:5 For many shall come in my name, saying, I am Christ; and shall deceive many.

Jesus is addressing His disciples specifically therefore this seems to be especially referring to those who would claim to be Jesus Himself returned. The ones who deceive those who reject Jesus the Christ anyway are bad enough but Christians need to be especially on guard against those who would attempt to deceive The Christ's followers whether they be weak or strong in the faith.

After the people had rejected the true Christ (Messiah) they were exposed to many false messiahs who succeeded in deceiving many. When many are deceived we should be especially cautious that we ourselves stay on the true path Christ called us to even as we attempt to sound the alarm for others to come to Christ, the only real Christ.

24:6 And ye shall hear of wars and rumours of wars: see that ye be not troubled: for all *these things* must come to pass, but the end is not yet.

The end shall not follow immediately.

Sin introduces wars, and they come from men's lusts. At times the nations are more distracted and wasted with wars than at other times. When Christ Jesus was born there was a general peace and shortly after He went out of the world there were general wars.

24:7 For nation shall rise against nation, and kingdom against kingdom: and there shall be famines, and pestilences, and earthquakes, in divers places.

The annals of Tacitus tell us how the Roman world was convulsed, before the destruction of Jerusalem, by rival claimants to the empire. The year of the four emperors preceded the siege of Jerusalem.

24:8 All these *are* the beginning of sorrows.

24:9 Then shall they deliver you up to be afflicted, and shall kill you: and ye shall be hated of all nations for my name's sake.

Prosperity gospel people beware: These are the actual words of Jesus. We ought not deceive ourselves with hopes that outward prosperity is guaranteed to us or that such a temporal kingdom as we may dream of has been promised. Some of us must be purified through tribulation to properly prepare us for the kingdom of God. We must take care not to needlessly expose ourselves to trouble and thereby put it upon our own head. Many are watching to see how we handle prosperity or calamity and it may be how we handle whatever comes our way which affects whether they shall be saved or no.

Groups of people that contend with one another will unite against us because of Whom we belong to.

24:10 And then shall many be offended, and shall betray one another, and shall hate one another.

24:11 And many false prophets shall rise, and shall deceive many.

Muhammad is just one of the many.

24:12 And because iniquity shall abound, the love of many shall wax cold.

24:13 But he that shall endure unto the end, the same shall be saved.

24:14 And this gospel of the kingdom shall be preached in all the world for a witness unto all nations; and then shall the end come.

24:15 When ye therefore shall see the abomination of desolation, spoken of by Daniel the prophet, stand in the holy place, (whoso readeth, let him understand:)

When Caligula came into power the Greek gods were fading from importance in the Roman psyche but he earnestly engaged in a campaign to promote them among the populace mainly because he lusted after becoming a permanent pagan god like Zeus or Apollo. About three years after becoming Emperor he ordered that every temple or place of worship in the Roman Empire make a statue of himself and worship it. Although the Jews' refusal initially enraged this madman, a wise counselor succeeded in dissuading him for a period of time. Unfortunately for the Jews their leadership didn't behave wisely though, and Caligula soon began toying with the idea of either destroying the Temple or personally entering its most sacred environs and force them to engage in Emperor Worship. However he met with death before he was able to attempt either.

If Jerusalem had not first profaned the crown of her holiness by rejecting Christ Jesus as an abomination, who would have been her salvation, she would not have experienced the desolation in AD 70.

The Jewish people, who were hoping that God would intervene and assist them had failed to realize the glory of God had departed their midst. In rebelling against the Romans and persecuting the Christians, who were their own brethren, the Jews were hastening their own demise, setting both God and man against them (see 1st Thessalonians 2:15).

When the Roman army came against the city there would be no safety anywhere in that vicinity. If the people were to only flee to the surrounding countryside it were not sufficient; only by escaping as instructed by Jesus from the area with all possible expediency could they hope to survive. They must flee to the mountains for the enemy was far too powerful and would give no quarter, having been stirred up to a high level of wrath.

While the Jewish Christians were fleeing the city, having heeded the warning sign, other Jews were flocking into the city seeking refuge all the while mocking the Christians. The Romans entered into the sanctuary to reduce to rubble that which the Jews held dear because the Jews had rejected that which God held dear (see Mark 12:1-12)

24:16 Then let them which be in Judaea flee into the mountains:

24:17 Let him which is on the housetop not come down to take any thing out of his house:

24:18 Neither let him which is in the field return back to take his clothes.

24:19 And woe unto them that are with child, and to them that give suck in those days!

24:20 But pray ye that your flight be not in the winter, neither on the sabbath day:

24:21 For then shall be great tribulation, such as was not since the beginning of the world to this time, no, nor ever shall be.

(see Daniel 12:1) It is a matter of literal fact that there was crowded into the period of the Jewish War of AD 70 a quantity and complication of suffering, perhaps unparalleled, at least, until the latter centuries, in the annals of human history; as the narrative of Josephus, examined carefully, shows.

24:22 And except those days should be shortened, there should no flesh be saved: but for the elect's sake those days shall be shortened.

In the case of the AD 70 desolation, if it had been allowed to continue for much longer there would have been no survivors. Likewise when the Tribulation period occurs just before the actual physical return of the Lord Jesus, the Christ, to this earth, conditions will be such that this verse will see its complete fulfillment. It is exceedingly difficult to comprehend how bad that will be, but we have been warned and are being warned.

24:23 Then if any man shall say unto you, Lo, here *is* Christ, or there; believe *it* not.

24:24 For there shall arise false Christs, and false prophets, and shall shew great signs and wonders; insomuch that, if *it were* possible, they shall deceive the very elect.

After the people had rejected the true Christ (Messiah) they were exposed to many false messiahs who succeeded in deceiving many. Whenever many are being deceived we should be especially cautious that we ourselves stay on the true path Christ called us to even as we attempt to sound the alarm for others to come to The Christ, the only real Christ.

24:25 Behold, I have told you before.

24:26 Wherefore if they shall say unto you, Behold, he is in the desert; go not forth: behold, *he is* in the secret chambers; believe *it* not.

24:27 For as the lightning cometh out of the east, and shineth even unto the west; so shall also the coming of the Son of man be.

24:28 For wheresoever the carcass is, there will the eagles be gathered together.

24:29 Immediately after the tribulation of those days shall the sun be darkened, and the moon shall not give her light, and the stars shall fall from heaven, and the powers of the heavens shall be shaken:

24:30 And then shall appear the sign of the Son of man in heaven: and then shall all the tribes of the earth mourn, and they shall see the Son of man coming in the clouds of heaven with power and great glory.

Through Christ the worlds were made. Through Christ salvation wrought. Through Christ judgment will be executed.

Too many wander along in the mistaken belief that God ignores their deeds resulting in good languishing while evil thrives. But He calls all to repentance while mercy may be obtained for the day will come when His judgment will be executed on all those who reject The Christ as the only way of salvation.

24:31 And he shall send his angels with a great sound of a trumpet, and they shall gather together his elect from the four winds, from one end of heaven to the other.

24:32 Now learn a parable of the fig tree; When his branch is yet tender, and putteth forth leaves, ye know that summer *is* nigh:

24:33 So likewise ye, when ye shall see all these things, know that it is near, *even* at the doors.

24:34 Verily I say unto you, This generation shall not pass, till all these things be fulfilled.

Interesting statement this. It could mean that the generation which sees Israel rebirthed in the land, which happened in May of AD 1948, will not pass away before the 2nd Advent of Christ Jesus takes place. On the other hand it possibly means the Jewish attitude of unbelief characterized by the rejection of their Messiah would continue until the day Jesus steps foot once again in Jerusalem. Some do believe, unfortunately most do not. While the former is the most likely meaning; we must take care to understand "Generation" or "nation" could be 40 years (past), 70 years (2018), or 100 years (2048) and Scripture passages can be brought forth in support of each; but the "when" is not actually given to us.

As the leaves of the fig tree indicate to us that summer is nigh, so events will occur which to the understanding mind will herald the Lord's return. Yet even these events do not tell us the when. Their purpose is to remind us that His return is at hand and we all need to be watching, properly engaged, and properly prepared.

24:35 Heaven and earth shall pass away, but my words shall not pass away.

24:36 But of that day and hour knoweth no *man,* no, not the angels of heaven, but my Father only.

It is easy to see why the close of the world should be reserved as a secret in the Father's mind. Had the church been told that it was near time wise, Christians would have been unfitted for the sober discharge of the duties of life: had the church been told that it was then remote time wise, such an assurance would have prompted sloth and negligence.

Yet we may all live, we must live, under a sense of the nearness of the Lord's return. We know this life is short and the day of our own personal accounting is not far off. We must never forget that we are all eternal creatures living a temporary human existence.

24:37 But as the days of Noe *were,* so shall also the coming of the Son of man be.

24:38 For as in the days that were before the flood they were eating and drinking, marrying and giving in marriage, until the day that Noe entered into the ark,

24:39 And knew not until the flood came, and took them all away; so shall also the coming of the Son of man be.

24:40 Then shall two be in the field; the one shall be taken, and the other left.

24:41 Two *women shall be* grinding at the mill; the one shall be taken, and the other left.

24:42 Watch therefore: for ye know not what hour your Lord doth come.

24:43 But know this, that if the goodman of the house had known in what watch the thief would come, he would have watched, and would not have suffered his house to be broken up.

24:44 Therefore be ye also ready: for in such an hour as ye think not the Son of man cometh.

24:45 Who then is a faithful and wise servant, whom his lord hath made ruler over his household, to give them meat in due season?

24:46 Blessed *is* that servant, whom his lord when he cometh shall find so doing.

24:47 Verily I say unto you, That he shall make him ruler over all his goods.

24:48 But and if that evil servant shall say in his heart, My lord delayeth his coming;

24:49 And shall begin to smite *his* fellowservants, and to eat and drink with the drunken;

24:50 The lord of that servant shall come in a day when he looketh not for *him,* and in an hour that he is not aware of,

24:51 And shall cut him asunder, and appoint *him* his portion with the hypocrites: there shall be weeping and gnashing of teeth.

We want to be wise stewards of whatever it is that we have been entrusted with, whether it be great or small. Followers of Jesus in every position of life are to work, watch, and pray.

CHAPTER TWENTY FIVE

25:1 Then shall the kingdom of heaven be likened unto ten virgins, which took their lamps, and went forth to meet the bridegroom.

25:2 And five of them were wise, and five *were* foolish.

25:3 They that *were* foolish took their lamps, and took no oil with them:

25:4 But the wise took oil in their vessels with their lamps.

25:5 While the bridegroom tarried, they all slumbered and slept.

25:6 And at midnight there was a cry made, Behold, the bridegroom cometh; go ye out to meet him.

25:7 Then all those virgins arose, and trimmed their lamps.

25:8 And the foolish said unto the wise, Give us of your oil; for our lamps are gone out.

25:9 But the wise answered, saying, *Not so;* lest there be not enough for us and you: but go ye rather to them that sell, and buy for yourselves.

25:10 And while they went to buy, the bridegroom came; and they that were ready went in with him to the marriage: and the door was shut.

25:11 Afterward came also the other virgins, saying, Lord, Lord, open to us.

25:12 But he answered and said, Verily I say unto you, I know you not.

25:13 Watch therefore, for ye know neither the day nor the hour wherein the Son of man cometh.

25:14 For *the kingdom of heaven is* as a man travelling into a far country, *who* called his own servants, and delivered unto them his goods.

25:15 And unto one he gave five talents, to another two, and to another one; to every man according to his several ability; and straightway took his journey.

25:16 Then he that had received the five talents went and traded with the same, and made *them* other five talents.

25:17 And likewise he that *had received* two, he also gained other two.

25:18 But he that had received one went and digged in the earth, and hid his lord's money.

25:19 After a long time the lord of those servants cometh, and reckoneth with them.

25:20 And so he that had received five talents came and brought other five talents, saying, Lord, thou deliveredst unto me five talents: behold, I have gained beside them five talents more.

25:21 His lord said unto him, Well done, *thou* good and faithful servant: thou hast been faithful over a few things, I will make thee ruler over many things: enter thou into the joy of thy lord.

25:22 He also that had received two talents came and said, Lord, thou deliveredst unto me two talents: behold, I have gained two other talents beside them.

25:23 His lord said unto him, Well done, good and faithful servant; thou hast been faithful over a few things, I will make thee ruler over many things: enter thou into the joy of thy lord.

25:24 Then he which had received the one talent came and said, Lord, I knew thee that thou art an hard man, reaping where thou hast not sown, and gathering where thou hast not strawed:

25:25 And I was afraid, and went and hid thy talent in the earth: lo, *there* thou hast *that is* thine.

25:26 His lord answered and said unto him, *Thou* wicked and slothful servant, thou knewest that I reap where I sowed not, and gather where I have not strawed:

25:27 Thou oughtest therefore to have put my money to the exchangers, and *then* at my coming I should have received mine own with usury.

25:28 Take therefore the talent from him, and give *it* unto him which hath ten talents.

25:29 For unto every one that hath shall be given, and he shall have abundance: but from him that hath not shall be taken away even that which he hath.

25:30 And cast ye the unprofitable servant into outer darkness: there shall be weeping and gnashing of teeth.

25:31 When the Son of man shall come in his glory, and all the holy angels with him, then shall he sit upon the throne of his glory:

25:32 And before him shall be gathered all nations: and he shall separate them one from another, as a shepherd divideth *his* sheep from the goats:

25:33 And he shall set the sheep on his right hand, but the goats on the left.

25:34 Then shall the King say unto them on his right hand, Come, ye blessed of my Father, inherit the kingdom prepared for you from the foundation of the world:

25:35 For I was an hungred, and ye gave me meat: I was thirsty, and ye gave me drink: I was a stranger, and ye took me in:

25:36 Naked, and ye clothed me: I was sick, and ye visited me: I was in prison, and ye came unto me.

25:37 Then shall the righteous answer him, saying, Lord, when saw we thee an hungred, and fed *thee?* or thirsty, and gave *thee* drink?

25:38 When saw we thee a stranger, and took *thee* in? or naked, and clothed *thee?*

25:39 Or when saw we thee sick, or in prison, and came unto thee?

25:40 And the King shall answer and say unto them, Verily I say unto you, Inasmuch as ye have done *it* unto one of the least of these my brethren, ye have done *it* unto me.

25:41 Then shall he say also unto them on the left hand. Depart from me, ye cursed, into everlasting fire, prepared for the devil and his angels:

25:42 For I was an hungred, and ye gave me no meat: I was thirsty, and ye gave me no drink:

25:43 I was a stranger, and ye took me not in: naked, and ye clothed me not: sick, and in prison, and ye visited me not.

25:44 Then shall they also answer him, saying, Lord, when saw we thee an hungred, or athirst, or a stranger, or naked, or sick, or in prison, and did not minister unto thee?

25:45 Then shall he answer them, saying, Verily I say unto you, Inasmuch as ye did *it* not to one of the least of these, ye did *it* not to me.

25:46 And these shall go away into everlasting punishment: but the righteous into life eternal.

CHAPTER TWENTY SIX

26:1 And it came to pass, when Jesus had finished all these sayings, he said unto his disciples,

26:2 Ye know that after two days is *the feast of* the passover, and the Son of man is betrayed to be crucified.

26:3 Then assembled together the chief priests, and the scribes, and the elders of the people, unto the palace of the high priest, who was called Caiaphas,

26:4 And consulted that they might take Jesus by subtilty, and kill *him.*

26:5 But they said, Not on the feast *day,* lest there be an uproar among the people.

26:6 Now when Jesus was in Bethany, in the house of Simon the leper,

26:7 There came unto him a woman having an alabaster box of very precious ointment, and poured it on his head, as he sat *at meat.*

26:8 But when his disciples saw *it,* they had indignation,

saying, To what purpose *is* this waste?

26:9 For this ointment might have been sold for much, and given to the poor.

26:10 When Jesus understood *it,* he said unto them, Why trouble ye the woman? for she hath wrought a good work upon me.

26:11 For ye have the poor always with you; but me ye have not always.

26:12 For in that she hath poured this ointment on my body, she did *it* for my burial.

26:13 Verily I say unto you, Wheresoever this gospel shall be preached in the whole world, *there* shall also this, that this woman hath done, be told for a memorial of her.

26:14 Then one of the twelve, called Judas Iscariot, went unto the chief priests,

26:15 And said *unto them,* What will ye give me, and I will deliver him unto you? And they covenanted with him for thirty pieces of silver.

26:16 And from that time he sought opportunity to betray him. It would appear that more than one of the disciples had murmured against this extravagant act by Mary but while the others are shamed and likely repented upon the rebuke from Jesus, Judas' covetousness caused him to get angry and actually approach Jesus' adversaries so that anger has been added to his crimes against Christ.

So while the chief priests were plotting how they might destroy Him, they found an unexpected ally in an angered unrepentant Apostle.

Mary's love for the Lord leads to a lovely act. Judas' love of money led to his loathsome act. A continued course of virtue or vice will lead to extraordinary acts of right conduct, or of misconduct. The end results would never have come to fruition if the chosen paths had not been long followed. Sin must be nipped in the bud early on or it will grow like a deadly cancer. Neither of these individuals had arrived at their respective points overnight.

26:17 Now the first *day* of the *feast of* unleavened bread the disciples came to Jesus, saying unto him, Where wilt thou that we prepare for thee to eat the passover?

26:18 And he said, Go into the city to such a man, and say unto him, The Master saith, My time is at hand; I will keep the passover at thy house with my disciples.

26:19 And the disciples did as Jesus had appointed them; and they made ready the passover.

26:20 Now when the even was come, he sat down with the twelve.

26:21 And as they did eat, he said, Verily I say unto you, that one of you shall betray me.

26:22 And they were exceeding sorrowful, and began every one of them to say unto him, Lord, is it I?

26:23 And he answered and said, He that dippeth *his* hand with me in the dish, the same shall betray me.

26:24 The Son of man goeth as it is written of him: but woe unto that man by whom the Son of man is betrayed! it had been good for that man if he had not been born.

26:25 Then Judas, which betrayed him, answered and said,

Master, is it I? He said unto him, Thou hast said.

Judas knew at this point that Jesus had to be fully aware of what he had already done and was planning to do. Jesus is also giving him one more chance to change his course of action.

God's permitting men to sin does not obligate them to sin and therefore it cannot be offered as an excuse for their guilt nor will it lessen their punishment.

26:26 And as they were eating, Jesus took bread, and blessed *it,* and brake *it,* and gave *it* to the disciples, and said, Take, eat; this is my body.

26:27 And he took the cup, and gave thanks, and gave *it* to them, saying, Drink ye all of it;

26:28 For this is my blood of the new testament, which is shed for many for the remission of sins.

26:29 But I say unto you, I will not drink henceforth of this fruit of the vine, until that day when I drink it new with you in my Father's kingdom.

26:30 And when they had sung an hymn, they went out into the mount of Olives.

26:31 Then saith Jesus unto them, All ye shall be offended because of me this night: for it is written, I will smite the shepherd, and the sheep of the flock shall be scattered abroad.

26:32 But after I am risen again, I will go before you into Galilee.

26:33 Peter answered and said unto him, Though all *men*

shall be offended because of thee, *yet* will I never be offended.

26:34 Jesus said unto him, Verily I say unto thee, That this night, before the cock crow, thou shalt deny me thrice.

26:35 Peter said unto him, Though I should die with thee, yet will I not deny thee. Likewise also said all the disciples.

It was a great spontaneous pep rally with bold words that would soon haunt each and every one of these Apostles because every one of them wound up "backsliding" that very night. Possibly if they had engaged themselves in prayer in the garden they would have fared better in the moment of crisis that caught them unaware. Unfortunately, for them, they still did not comprehend what Jesus had been trying to tell them over the last few months. How many times have we, ourselves, failed to be as properly prepared spiritually as we ought to have been at certain times because of our own lack of proper preparation in prayer or the perusal of the Scriptures?

26:36 Then cometh Jesus with them unto a place called Gethsemane, and saith unto the disciples, Sit ye here, while I go and pray yonder.

26:37 And he took with him Peter and the two sons of Zebedee, and began to be sorrowful and very heavy.

26:38 Then saith he unto them, My soul is exceeding sorrowful, even unto death: tarry ye here, and watch with me.

26:39 And he went a little further, and fell on his face, and prayed, saying, O my Father, if it be possible, let this cup pass from me: nevertheless not as I will, but as thou *wilt*.

26:40 And he cometh unto the disciples, and findeth them asleep, and saith unto Peter, What, could ye not watch with me one hour?

26:41 Watch and pray, that ye enter not into temptation: the spirit indeed *is* willing, but the flesh *is* weak.

26:42 He went away again the second time, and prayed, saying, O my Father, if this cup may not pass away from me, except I drink it, thy will be done.

26:43 And he came and found them asleep again: for their eyes were heavy.

26:44 And he left them, and went away again, and prayed the third time, saying the same words.

26:45 Then cometh he to his disciples, and saith unto them, Sleep on now, and take *your* rest: behold, the hour is at hand, and the Son of man is betrayed into the hands of sinners.

26:46 Rise, let us be going: behold, he is at hand that doth betray me.

    The man who prayed in anguish beneath the trees comes forth in tranquility and He gave Himself up to death for us all. It is a full moon and He could quite easily have escaped from the hands of His enemies but He walks toward them and meets them. He gives one flash of power to show that even now they are too weak to take Him against His will.

26:47 And while he yet spake, lo, Judas, one of the twelve, came, and with him a great multitude with swords and staves, from the chief priests and elders of the people.

26:48 Now he that betrayed him gave them a sign, saying,

Whomsoever I shall kiss, that same is he: hold him fast.

26:49 And forthwith he came to Jesus, and said, Hail, master; and kissed him.

26:50 And Jesus said unto him, Friend, wherefore art thou come? Then came they, and laid hands on Jesus, and took him.

26:51 And, behold, one of them which were with Jesus stretched out *his* hand, and drew his sword, and struck a servant of the high priest's, and smote off his ear.

26:52 Then said Jesus unto him, Put up again thy sword into his place: for all they that take the sword shall perish with the sword.

26:53 Thinkest thou that I cannot now pray to my Father, and he shall presently give me more than twelve legions of angels?

26:54 But how then shall the scriptures be fulfilled, that thus it must be?

26:55 In that same hour said Jesus to the multitudes, Are ye come out as against a thief with swords and staves for to take me? I sat daily with you teaching in the temple, and ye laid no hold on me.

26:56 But all this was done, that the scriptures of the prophets might be fulfilled. Then all the disciples forsook him, and fled.

26:57 And they that had laid hold on Jesus led *him* away to Caiaphas the high priest, where the scribes and the elders were assembled.

26:58 But Peter followed him afar off unto the high priest's palace, and went in, and sat with the servants, to see the end.

26:59 Now the chief priests, and elders, and all the council, sought false witness against Jesus, to put him to death;

    Probably paid false witnesses, but they couldn't get their stories straight which may be because they themselves had been hastily roused from sleep and put on the spot too quickly ccordinate their false stories.

26:60 But found none: yea, though many false witnesses came, *yet* found they none. At the last came two false witnesses,

26:61 And said, This *fellow* said, I am able to destroy the temple of God, and to build it in three days.

26:62 And the high priest arose, and said unto him, Answerest thou nothing? what *is it which* these witness against thee?

26:63 But Jesus held his peace. And the high priest answered and said unto him, I adjure thee by the living God, that thou tell us whether thou be the Christ, the Son of God.

26:64 Jesus saith unto him, Thou hast said: nevertheless I say unto you, Hereafter shall ye see the Son of man sitting on the right hand of power, and coming in the clouds of heaven.

26:65 Then the high priest rent his clothes, saying, He hath spoken blasphemy; what further need have we of witnesses? behold, now ye have heard his blasphemy.

26:66 What think ye? They answered and said, He is guilty

of death.

26:67 Then did they spit in his face, and buffeted him; and others smote *him* with the palms of their hands,

26:68 Saying, Prophesy unto us, thou Christ, Who is he that smote thee?

26:69 Now Peter sat without in the palace: and a damsel came unto him, saying, Thou also wast with Jesus of Galilee.

26:70 But he denied before *them* all, saying, I know not what thou sayest.

26:71 And when he was gone out into the porch, another *maid* saw him, and said unto them that were there, This *fellow* was also with Jesus of Nazareth.

26:72 And again he denied with an oath, I do not know the man.

26:73 And after a while came unto *him* they that stood by, and said to Peter, Surely thou also art *one* of them; for thy speech betrayeth thee.

26:74 Then began he to curse and to swear, *saying,* I know not the man. And immediately the cock crew.

26:75 And Peter remembered the word of Jesus, which said unto him, Before the cock crow, thou shalt deny me thrice. And he went out, and wept bitterly.

CHAPTER TWENTY SEVEN

27:1 When the morning was come, all the chief priests and elders of the people took counsel against Jesus to put him to death:

27:2 And when they had bound him, they led *him* away, and delivered him to Pontius Pilate the governor.

27:3 Then Judas, which had betrayed him, when he saw that he was condemned, repented himself, and brought again the thirty pieces of silver to the chief priests and elders,

27:4 Saying, I have sinned in that I have betrayed the innocent blood. And they said, What *is that* to us? see thou *to that.*

27:5 And he cast down the pieces of silver in the temple, and departed, and went and hanged himself.

27:6 And the chief priests took the silver pieces, and said, It is not lawful for to put them into the treasury, because it is the price of blood.

27:7 And they took counsel, and bought with them the

potter's field, to bury strangers in.

27:8 Wherefore that field was called, The field of blood, unto this day.

27:9 Then was fulfilled that which was spoken by Jeremy the prophet, saying, And they took the thirty pieces of silver, the price of him that was valued, whom they of the children of Israel did value;

27:10 And gave them for the potter's field, as the Lord appointed me.

27:11 And Jesus stood before the governor: and the governor asked him, saying, Art thou the King of the Jews? And Jesus said unto him, Thou sayest.

Christ gave Pilate a fairly direct answer, but He would not answer the accusers because the things they alleged were known by themselves to be false, even Pilate himself was convinced they were false. This isn't Pilate's first encounter with these people. However, in a sense, Jesus gave Pilate a strange answer because the indirectness of this direct answer won't allow Pilate to easily discharge the case before him.

To a casual observer Jesus is bound before Pilate but the truth of the matter is that Pilate was the prisoner that day. Pilate had made a couple of missteps which had resulted in his being stuck in this assignment. Then in an effort to quench the rebellious spirit of this people he had taken strong measures which would have worked in most other places, but they had backfired here. Therefore, Pilate was stuck between a rock and a hard place; he desperately wanted to release Jesus but he could not do so without risking losing his own life. "Coincidentally," the Priests had actually willingly surrendered their authority to execute not very many months before. Any ordinary Jew Pilate could have and would have executed with barely a second thought but Pilate knew that this Jesus was no ordinary man even if he couldn't quite comprehend why.

27:12 And when he was accused of the chief priests and elders, he answered nothing.

27:13 Then said Pilate unto him, Hearest thou not how many things they witness against thee?

27:14 And he answered to him never a word; insomuch that the governor marvelled greatly.

Such an unusual prisoner. Pilate had tried to pass the buck but that had not worked out. So many details and even those supplied should grab our attention and make us realize that there is a whole lot more than meets the eye going on here. But what has been documented for us is that which we most need to know. Understand this, Jesus could very easily have secured His release without even having to call upon the heavenly host. He is the one who is in control of everything, not the priests, and certainly not Pilate.

In the spiritual realm, the demons are trembling in terror and the angels are agitated and they ready to destroy all humankind, not to mention the demonic powers, but they are being restrained by the hand of the one true God.

27:15 Now at *that* feast the governor was wont to release unto the people a prisoner, whom they would.

It was a custom to release a prisoner at the Passover feast, not always observed, but the crowd that was/had gathered would have been Barabbas' friends and cohorts while most of those who were of a favorable opinion towards Jesus probably were still completely unaware of the arrest or what was happening at Pilate's hall. The disciples were in hiding and therefore they had not spread the alarm. It is true crowds are often fickle but this little mob was already predisposed to asking for Barabbas and the Priests had an unexpected ally in them. However Pilate tried to appeal to the people in an effort to overrule the Priests and appears to have offered Jesus as well after they had requested Barabbas. The Priests acted quickly and incited the crowd to scream "Crucify Him." Later, many in the crowd may have wondered "What happened?"

27:16 And they had then a notable prisoner, called Barabbas.

27:17 Therefore when they were gathered together, Pilate said unto them, Whom will ye that I release unto you? Barabbas, or Jesus which is called Christ?

27:18 For he knew that for envy they had delivered him.

27:19 When he was set down on the judgment seat, his wife sent unto him, saying, Have thou nothing to do with that just man: for I have suffered many things this day in a dream because of him.

27:20 But the chief priests and elders persuaded the multitude that they should ask Barabbas, and destroy Jesus.

If ever an error could be excused by the plea of authority, and the duty of submission to constituted leaders, it was this error. They followed men who sat in Moses' seat, and who were thus entitled, according to Jesus Himself, to be obeyed. Yet that authority has not relieved the Hebrew people from the wrath that came upon them to the uttermost. The salvation they desired was not moral elevation or spiritual life, and so, in their opinion, Jesus had nothing to bestow upon them; they refused the Just and Holy One. What they wanted was the world, the position of power which Rome held, and which they fondly still hoped to be theirs.

27:21 The governor answered and said unto them, Whether of the twain will ye that I release unto you? They said, Barabbas.

27:22 Pilate saith unto them, What shall I do then with Jesus which is called Christ? *They* all say unto him, Let him be crucified.

In other words, "This is your lucky day, ask now and I'll give you both men." The conscience of Pilate struggled hard, aided by superstitious fear. The silence of Jesus only added to that. His wife's dream added even more stress. He had already incurred imperial censure and could be ruined if accused of releasing a conspirator against Caesar. His only hope was the custom of releasing a prisoner at Passover and he was apparently hoping to claim the clamor of the crowd caused him to release two prisoners to them instead of the customary one.

27:23 And the governor said, Why, what evil hath he done? But they cried out the more, saying, Let him be crucified.

If not for the community agitators the people might have given more careful thought. The popular hero is a mirror which reflects the popular mind but not necessarily the majority. The Priests had agitated the crowd to respond without thinking.

Jesus had taught things they really did not want to hear. They were interested in power over the secular sector; a life reflecting the beauty of holiness has little appeal, even in our day. The moral midget mohammed gets accepted by immoral multitudes while the mighty Messiah who manifested miracles gets maligned by multitudes. It is better to be condemned by the world with Jesus than be accepted with such a one as the world often wants.

That day they requested and received the son of the father (Bar abbas) and refused to receive the Son of the Father.

27:24 When Pilate saw that he could prevail nothing, but *that* rather a tumult was made, he took water, and washed *his* hands before the multitude, saying, I am innocent of the blood of this just person: see ye *to it.*

In an effort to calm the crowd, Pilate consents to their stated will, lest a full-fledged riot break out. His name is ill spoken of in the creed of Christendom – "Crucified under Pontius Pilate," but it is only partly deserved.

One is tempted to pity the feeble judge, the only person who is known to have attempted to rescue Jesus, but Pilate was entrapped by his old faults. Some seeds he had sown had come to fruition. No accomplice in this frightful crime is so suggesting of a warning to hearts which are not entirely hardened.

But our pity tends to dry up and blow away like chaff when we remember that this governor, having borne witness to the perfect innocence of Jesus, in order to save himself from danger, yielded Him up to die. Therefore Pilate prostituted justice for his own ends just like many liberal/progressive politicians-justices-people do today. Pilate's crime was great but his guilt is measured by his own light and that was small.

He did not follow the dawning of light that could have led him to know Jesus as savior that day. A bit more light would shine in his face before the day was out.

27:25 Then answered all the people, and said, His blood *be* on us, and on our children.

27:26 Then released he Barabbas unto them: and when he had scourged Jesus, he delivered *him* to be crucified.

27:27 Then the soldiers of the governor took Jesus into the common hall, and gathered unto him the whole band *of soldiers.*

27:28 And they stripped him, and put on him a scarlet robe.

27:29 And when they had platted a crown of thorns, they put *it* upon his head, and a reed in his right hand: and they bowed the knee before him, and mocked him, saying, Hail, King of the Jews!

27:30 And they spit upon him, and took the reed, and smote him on the head.

27:31 And after that they had mocked him, they took the robe off from him, and put his own raiment on him, and led him away to crucify *him.*

27:32 And as they came out, they found a man of Cyrene, Simon by name: him they compelled to bear his cross.

27:33 And when they were come unto a place called Golgotha, that is to say, a place of a skull,

27:34 They gave him vinegar to drink mingled with gall: and when he had tasted *thereof,* he would not drink.

Most likely the primary purpose of this stupefying drink was to make the soldiers' job of nailing the criminal to the cross a little bit easier because the undrugged prisoner would most certainly be endowed with almost superhuman strength once the excruciatingly painful process commenced.

Jesus had resolved to die with His mental vision clear and calm. The drink actually could have weakened His resolve to remain on the cross.

27:35 And they crucified him, and parted his garments, casting lots: that it might be fulfilled which was spoken by the prophet, They parted my garments among them, and upon my vesture did they cast lots.

27:36 And sitting down they watched him there;

27:37 And set up over his head his accusation written, THIS IS JESUS THE KING OF THE JEWS.

27:38 Then were there two thieves crucified with him, one on the right hand, and another on the left.

27:39 And they that passed by reviled him, wagging their heads,

27:40 And saying, Thou that destroyest the temple, and buildest *it* in three days, save thyself. If thou be the Son of God, come down from the cross.

The passers-by were probably Jews who intended to keep the Passover inside the city. Outside they paused long enough to hurl insults at God's Paschal Lamb. Most are ignorant but some are willfully blind.

They misquote Him as threatening to destroy their temple and to rebuild it in three days. The priests' words to Pilate prove they knew what He meant by what He actually said.

27:41 Likewise also the chief priests mocking *him,* with the scribes and elders, said,

27:42 He saved others; himself he cannot save. If he be the King of Israel, let him now come down from the cross, and we will believe him.

In their mocking, these foolishly ignorant people accidentally told the truth; if Jesus had saved Himself then He would not have been able to save others. They would have believed Him, maybe but probably not, but it would not have done them one iota of good.

They thought the nails held Him up there but those nails were as nothing; it was love, the one true God loves you and that is why the one true God permitted this to happen. That is why the one true God gets so angry at those who disbelieve in Jesus, the holy one from the one true God.

If Jesus' resolve to stay would have failed and He had come down the people would have probably attempted to manufacture another reason not to believe but it would not have mattered anyway for salvation's wondrous plan would have failed. But Jesus did provide an even more wondrous sign in that He rose again from the grave just and He had said He would.

27:43 He trusted in God; let him deliver him now, if he will have him: for he said, I am the Son of God.

27:44 The thieves also, which were crucified with him, cast the same in his teeth.

27:45 Now from the sixth hour there was darkness over all the land unto the ninth hour.

This three hour darkness should have caused the enemies of Christ to understand that He was the light of the world, no mere solar eclipse can last that long, and they, of all people, should have remembered the events that led up to the first Passover observance when the darkness came upon the Egyptians.

27:46 And about the ninth hour Jesus cried with a loud voice, saying, Eli, Eli, lama sabachthani? that is to say, My God, my God, why hast thou forsaken me?

27:47 Some of them that stood there, when they heard *that,* said, This *man* calleth for Elias.

27:48 And straightway one of them ran, and took a sponge, and filled *it* with vinegar, and put *it* on a reed, and gave him to drink.

27:49 The rest said, Let be, let us see whether Elias will come to save him.

27:50 Jesus, when he had cried again with a loud voice, yielded up the ghost.

27:51 And, behold, the veil of the temple was rent in twain from the top to the bottom; and the earth did quake, and the rocks rent;

At the same instant that Jesus died the veil to the holy of holies was torn from top to bottom. This spoke terror to the unbelieving Jews and was a sign of the demolition of their system. They would attempt to dismiss this rending of the veil as having been caused by the earthquake and they recorded that claim in the Talmud.

The holy of holies of Herod's Temple contained only a large stone, on which the high priest sprinkled blood on the day of atonement, occupying the place where the ark with the mercy-seat was supposed to be. It is believed that the ark is currently in a special place in Africa and will be transported from there to the new temple when it is built and ready to receive it.

This rending of the veil at the precise time that Jesus expires on the cross speaks comfort to all who believe in the Christ which includes, "a great number of the priests [who] were obedient to the faith" (Acts 6:7). It signifies a new and living way into the holy place through the blood of Jesus.

27:52 And the graves were opened; and many bodies of the saints which slept arose,

27:53 And came out of the graves after his resurrection, and went into the holy city, and appeared unto many.

27:54 Now when the centurion, and they that were with him, watching Jesus, saw the earthquake, and those things that were done, they feared greatly, saying, Truly this was the Son of God.

More probably his statement should be translated "A son of god," for he does not yet understand what has happened but he knows this was no ordinary man and he is not likely to rest until he finds out why this man is so different than all other men and exactly who He is. Others also changed their opinions regarding Jesus because of the events at Golgotha. No doubt, many who had come from Jerusalem to see the spectacle returned in sorrow and fear, wondering what it all meant. Perhaps as he thoughtfully went back to his barrack that evening the process began which led him to true faith. Sadly, others, who already had refused to see, still failed to see.

27:55 And many women were there beholding afar off, which followed Jesus from Galilee, ministering unto him:

27:56 Among which was Mary Magdalene, and Mary the mother of James and Joses, and the mother of Zebedee's children.

27:57 When the even was come, there came a rich man of Arimathaea, named Joseph, who also himself was Jesus' disciple:

27:58 He went to Pilate, and begged the body of Jesus. Then Pilate commanded the body to be delivered.

27:59 And when Joseph had taken the body, he wrapped it in a clean linen cloth,

27:60 And laid it in his own new tomb, which he had hewn out in the rock: and he rolled a great stone to the door of the sepulchre, and departed.

27:61 And there was Mary Magdalene, and the other Mary, sitting over against the sepulchre.

27:62 Now the next day, that followed the day of the preparation, the chief priests and Pharisees came together unto Pilate,

27:63 Saying, Sir, we remember that that deceiver said, while he was yet alive, After three days I will rise again.

27:64 Command therefore that the sepulchre be made sure until the third day, lest his disciples come by night, and steal him away, and say unto the people, He is risen from the dead: so the last error shall be worse than the first.

27:65 Pilate said unto them, Ye have a watch: go your way,

make *it* as sure as ye can.

27:66 So they went, and made the sepulchre sure, sealing the stone, and setting a watch.

The centurion would have given a full accounting: the darkness, the words uttered by Jesus, the earthquake's timing and how He had dismissed His spirit. Therefore I am of the opinion that when the priests requested a guard be placed at the tomb Pilate very nearly grabbed his sword to run them through with it. At any rate, Pilate is alarmed enough to assign Roman soldiers to seal and guard the tomb. Some have tried, in a blatant effort to dismiss the resurrection, to claim they were merely temple guards. These were real Roman soldiers; probably the best and most trusted that Pilate had on hand, as the Scripture makes quite clear to anyone with eyes to see. The penalty for a Roman soldier caught sleeping on duty was death on the spot, therefore they did not.

CHAPTER TWENTY EIGHT

28:1 In the end of the sabbath, as it began to dawn toward the first *day* of the week, came Mary Magdalene and the other Mary to see the sepulchre.

The women were bringing spices to further anoint the body of Christ; they were aware of the copious amount of spices already applied by Nicodemus. His were probably of the dry variety while theirs was of the perfumed oil type. Particular notice should be taken that the respect which others have shown The Christ should never hinder us from doing our part.

28:2 And, behold, there was a great earthquake: for the angel of the Lord descended from heaven, and came and rolled back the stone from the door, and sat upon it.

28:3 His countenance was like lightning, and his raiment white as snow:

28:4 And for fear of him the keepers did shake, and became as dead *men.*

28:5 And the angel answered and said unto the women,

Fear not ye: for I know that ye seek Jesus, which was crucified.

28:6 He is not here: for he is risen, as he said. Come, see the place where the Lord lay.

The angel appeared in the likeness of a young man and his presence and appearance was intended to encourage them but still they were quite frightened. So many times, that which should be encouraging and comforting to us, because of our own misapprehensions and mistakes, winds up being a terror to us.

He attempts to allay their fears by assuring them that there is cause for celebration in spite of, and because of, the events of the last few days. As angels rejoice in the conversion of sinners, so do they also in the consolation of saints. We must not dwell upon the sad circumstances of His crucifixion so as to be unable to believe in the Joyful fact of His Resurrection. The glory of His resurrection wipes away all the reproach of His sufferings

Most of Mohammad's followers reject the resurrection and therefore cannot comprehend the cross or Jesus' followers commemorating the Christ who was crucified and now lives forever; for them Jesus was only a prophet while for us, who believe, He is the living Savior. He could be their Savior too if they would only stop being disbelievers

Jesus has never drawn a veil over His sufferings nor shied away from having His cross spoken of. Instead of anointing or commemorating a corpse, we rejoice in a resurrection.

A real birth; a real life; a real death; a real resurrection.

28:7 And go quickly, and tell his disciples that he is risen from the dead; and, behold, he goeth before you into Galilee; there shall ye see him: lo, I have told you.

This verse should give each one of us encouragement whenever we err or flat out fail; Jesus still cares and will welcome His wandering child back into the fold. Christ is not ashamed to own His poor defeated disciples; He takes care to have them notified. Peter needs especial encouragement and assurance that he was not completely castaway by The Christ.

28:8 And they departed quickly from the sepulchre with fear and great joy; and did run to bring his disciples word.

28:9 And as they went to tell his disciples, behold, Jesus met them, saying, All hail. And they came and held him by the feet, and worshipped him.

28:10 Then said Jesus unto them, Be not afraid: go tell my brethren that they go into Galilee, and there shall they see me.

28:11 Now when they were going, behold, some of the watch came into the city, and shewed unto the chief priests all the things that were done.

28:12 And when they were assembled with the elders, and had taken counsel, they gave large money unto the soldiers,

28:13 Saying, Say ye, His disciples came by night, and stole him *away* while we slept.

28:14 And if this come to the governor's ears, we will persuade him, and secure you.

28:15 So they took the money, and did as they were taught: and this saying is commonly reported among the Jews until this day.

28:16 Then the eleven disciples went away into Galilee, into a mountain where Jesus had appointed them.

28:17 And when they saw him, they worshipped him: but some doubted.

28:18 And Jesus came and spake unto them, saying, All power is given unto me in heaven and in earth.

28:19 Go ye therefore, and teach all nations, baptizing them in the name of the Father, and of the Son, and of the Holy Ghost:

Proclaim the glad tidings of Christ crucified and raised from the dead to every man, woman, and child on the face of the planet. For those who reject (disbelieve) it, John 3:18 applies and for those who accept (believe) it, John 3:16 applies. It's a whosoever won't and a whosoever will thing.

28:20 Teaching them to observe all things whatsoever I have commanded you: and, lo, I am with you alway, *even* unto the end of the world. Amen.

ABOUT THE AUTHOR

Pastor Ward Clinton has been included in the Heritage Registry of Who's Who, a New York based biographical publication which selects and distinguishes individuals throughout North America who have attained a recognizable degree of success in their field of endeavor. Pastor Clinton has dedicated most of his life to helping others. He has given 20 years to his country in military service and is a veteran of at least 4 wars, bracketed by Vietnam and Gulf War One. While on active military duty he participated in restoration work on orphanages in South Korea and the Philippines, including an elementary school in the Philippines. He has received numerous awards and letters of commendation.

While stationed in Guam, USA he was an Associate Pastor. After leaving the Navy he found his calling in the full-time ministry of the gospel of Jesus Christ enrolling in 1993 at Southern Nazarene University while working with the homeless in Oklahoma City. He pastored a church in Western Kansas after Oklahoma. Certain members of the Micronesia Church of The Nazarene routinely sent him invites to return to ministry in the tropical island of Guam every January for many years after he had left.

Made in the USA
Charleston, SC
19 April 2016